WAKING UP IN HEAVEN

WAKING UP
in *Heaven*

Living
with Purpose
through
Afterlife Wisdom

by ELLEN WIER

CARLSBAD CALIFORNIA

WAKING UP:

Living with Purpose Through Afterlife Wisdom

© 2024 Ellen Wier

Published by the author in affiliation with
Fearless Literary Services • Assisted Publishing

ISBN: 979-8-218-39345-8

LIBRARY OF CONGRESS CONTROL NUMBER:
2024907366

COVER DESIGN:
Beverly Haney

PRODUCTION & MANAGEMENT
D. Patrick Miller • Fearless Literary
www.fearlessbooks.com

The following essential oils and essential oil blends presented in
this book are trademarks of Young Living Essential Oils, LLC:

Divine Release™
Freedom™
Joy™
T.R. Care™
Transformation™

TABLE OF CONTENTS

For my kids, who opened
my eyes to the purest form of love.

For my parents, who showed me the strength
and warmth of love through their actions.

And for Neil, who taught me the warmth
and wonder of a loving relationship.

This book is dedicated to you, for
teaching me the many dimensions of love.

PREFACE

IN THE blink of an eye, my world changed. From coma to
the realm of light and back, music was the force that
brought me home. At the tender age of twelve, I encountered
the unfathomable: a near-death experience that unveiled the
vast light of the universe and the music that threads it together. This celestial symphony was not just heard but felt, rever-
berating through the very essence of my being. It was in this
liminal space between worlds that I discovered my purpose
and the healing power of sound.

Music is a universal language, a vibrational bridge connecting the physical and the spiritual. Music did not just heal
me; it transformed me. It led me on a path to become a music
therapist, a spiritual coach, and a guide for those seeking to
connect with their higher selves through the embrace of high-
frequency modalities.

Through my work, I have had the privilege of touching the
lives of many, from celebrities to seekers of light, aiding their
journey towards self-discovery, healing, and transcendence.
Each encounter, each session, is a testament to the power of

sound to alter states of consciousness, to connect us to our own higher knowing, to heal, and to empower the soul to soar.

This book is not just a narrative; it's an invitation to embark on a profound journey of self-discovery and transformation. Rooted in sound healing, transpersonal psychology, and spiritual awakening, it weaves together insights, practices, and testimonies to illuminate the path to self-healing and spiritual expansion. Through the lens of my personal journey and the lessons learned along the way, this teaching memoir aims to guide you towards connecting with your own high presence.

As you turn these pages, you are encouraged to explore the depths of your own soul, unlock the healing potential within, and connect with the infinite wisdom of the universe. This journey is one of returning to your essence, embracing your inner light, and living with a profound sense of presence in every moment. Let the symphony of your soul guide you. Welcome to the journey.

CHAPTER 1

A Journey to Heaven and Back

Music: the cosmic dance of sound
unites our bodies with the rhythms of creation

IREMEMBER it vividly: Light wrapped around me like a weighted blanket as Source welcomed me home. My first glimpse of Heaven showed a flash of trees in turquoise hues with a brightly colored pastel stream flowing in the distance. It reminded me a bit of Earth, but the colors were more muted. I didn't see any other beings, but I felt them around me in the form of love. As my ears acclimated to this place, an otherworldly music mesmerized me. This music of the spheres swirled around me in a healing dance of sound. Time seemed to stop. There was no fear, no pain, nor any other human sensation. I was immersed in wholeness; somehow I was everything.

The trees and stream then quickly dissipated into an intense golden light, as bright as the sun itself. This "light blanket" charged and flooded my soul, until I slowly melted into the fullness of it. I then became part of this luminous

Presence, one with the heart of God. I had come Home.

That day, as my physical body lay comatose, my life changed forever. While my human form remained dormant, my soul embarked on a blissful journey through Heaven. I stood at the precipice of a challenging spiritual choice: Would I continue on in this life, or remain in the realm of the Divine?

In Heaven, I came to realize that I chose to come into this embodiment for a greater purpose. With the wisdom of countless lifetimes, millions of ancestors, and Source at my fingertips, I arrived on this earth fully equipped to fulfill my mission. My rebirth in Heaven marked the beginning of my journey to show others how to manifest Heaven on Earth.

I was clear about so many things when I awoke from the coma in the Intensive Care Unit. When I opened my eyes, I knew with absolute certainty what I was here to do. I knew it because just before I returned to my physical body, I *chose my purpose.* Heaven gave me all the wisdom I needed to live a fulfilled and joyful life. I came back understanding humanity's purpose on Earth and our full potential. To this day, the wisdom from the light realm guides my path. As I continue to share my experiences with the world, I consciously build my connection to my God Presence, which allows even more messages to flow.

Living with this awareness has taught me to access the inherent power we all possess, enabling me to help my clients receive their own spiritual messages. While universal messages vary for each individual, their purpose is to remind us of our spiritual light and the wisdom within. In this book, I'll lead you through my awakening journey and offer guidance to help you enhance your intuitive skills. I'll share techniques for accessing this awareness, allowing you to lead a purposeful, loving, and fulfilling life through co-creating with the Divine.

A Near-Death Experience (NDE)

At twelve years old, I loved riding horses. During one lesson, the cinch, which is the belt that holds the saddle on the horse, wasn't tight enough. Horses are known to swell their bellies, as they don't like the tightness of the cinches. So, they breathe in air and hold it until the cinch is fastened on, and then exhale to create space between the cinch and their belly for comfort. If the rider isn't aware of this and doesn't adjust the tightness after an exhale, the saddle can become loose after a short time of riding.

That's what happened to me. With a loose cinch, the saddle slipped to the side with me in it as I held on for dear life. I dropped under the belly of the horse before falling off completely. As I hit the ground, the horse, startled, reared up, and delivered a forceful kick to my right temple which instantly plunged me into unconsciousness.

Rushed to one hospital, I was soon transferred to another, Hillcrest Baptist Medical Center in Waco, Texas. The medical team recommended the move because of Hillcrest's renowned neurological specialists, one of whom had treated President John F. Kennedy. The decision to transfer to Hillcrest Hospital proved to be pivotal, as their esteemed neurological team proposed interventions that laid the groundwork for my NDE.

Despite the fact that I was deep in a coma, the neurological team encouraged my parents to play movies at my bedside to try to stimulate my brain. After visiting hours in the Intensive Care Unit (ICU) had ended, they would play home movies and cartoons for me. My mother, who practically lived at the hospital throughout my stay, would spend time in the cafeteria when visiting hours for the Intensive Care Unit were over. Her unwavering hope for my recovery was clear when she turned away the priest who had arrived to administer last rites. She told him that his services were not needed. Her child would not die.

My parents played home movies and cartoons, hoping to reach me with familiar content. However, there came a day when my parents chose to play a Disney movie that featured classical music. It was the melodies of this film's musical score that brought the true magic to this experience, playing a significant role in my journey to wakefulness. In the end, the music is the hero of my story.

Sidelined from everyday happenings in the human world, I lay in a coma in the intensive care unit (ICU) . At first, there was a sense of nothingness — until it changed. All at once nothingness shifted into a vision of myself on a wooden raft, navigating a river of pink clouds. The clouds billowed up on the shore of the cloud river, each "bank" representing a place. I tried to make sense of where I was, not realizing I was losing connection to my thinking mind. I let everything go when I realized I was safe. I felt fully protected and loved. It was as if I were looking through the lens of a camera, once removed yet fully present.

I saw Jesus standing before me, dressed in plain white robes. His eyes were pools of love and grace, and I was captivated by their beauty. To my left stood an adult, bald man, dressed in long brown robes. His energy was comforting, strong, and grounded, even though he never communicated directly with me. Only Jesus communicated with me, and that was through our thoughts. In that moment, I didn't know who the man in the brown robes was, but I knew he was significant. In due time, I would come to recognize his identity, and he would assume a significant role in shaping my life.

On the raft I felt full acceptance and an overwhelming sense of love. Yet, my time there was brief. Before long, my soul lifted toward a golden light: a resplendent, radiant brilliance accompanied by a symphony of music from unseen instruments. It felt like a weighted blanket around me. The golden light felt *full*, radiating complete love. I left my body. I was part of something greater. I became one with the unconditional love, peace, and joy of the universe—a truly exhilarating experience. I could have been there a day, a year, or even many lifetimes. On Earth it was five days, but on the other side, time didn't exist.

After experiencing this light from which we came, I went back to the raft with a profound sense of transformation.

I would no longer be the twelve-year-old girl who entered Heaven. I now carried the wisdom of the light. I stood on the raft in front of Jesus again, and instantly began receiving divine downloads — infusions of information from beyond. These messages still serve as a roadmap to my future, and they are the messages I came back to share with others.

Jesus' words filled my head as he communicated telepathically. I knew that I had a choice to make. There was no right or wrong, and I knew that everything would be alright regardless of which route I chose. The choice was to stay in the place of light or return to Earth and live out my life. Imagine that choice for an instant. I had just experienced the most profound *love* I had ever known, immersed in absolute oneness. I wanted to feel it again, so part of me wanted greatly to stay.

Then, as if by design, I received more downloads, this time about my family. The path of my loved ones played out in front of me. I saw that life would move on without me — but I also saw that if I stayed on the other side, my father wouldn't fully actualize his purpose in this life. I was also shown the trajectory of my brothers' lives and how they would be affected in relationships, with the weight of a lingering loss affecting them throughout their lifetimes.

This new information came through clearly, with no emotions attached. This lack of emotional impact was a gift. It gave me the opportunity to use the power of my own free will, uninfluenced by human limitation. There were truly no strings attached to the choice. The concept of free will — one of the core lessons that I will explore in this book — seemed to be a paramount factor in my spiritual evolution.

I absorbed this information about the lives of my family before Jesus asked me: "Would you like to stay, or go back to complete your life on Earth?"

I made the choice to live — of my own free will and guided by the power of love. This is when everything started to accelerate. As soon as I made the choice, I was flooded with gifts of knowledge and insight about human existence. I received revelations about our purpose, the significance of our existence in this moment, and the true essence of life. These downloads were so powerful that my life is still guided by them, and I look forward to sharing them later in this book.

Choosing Life with Gratitude

When I made the choice to live, I was immediately flooded with gratitude, as if the cosmos were celebrating along with me. I was so overwhelmed with gratitude that I made a sacred vow. I vowed that every moment in my life would *count*. I would live life to the fullest, make every moment matter, and give thanks for every second that I got to *live*.

Then I received my purpose with profound clarity. I vowed that I would return to Earth to *heal people with music*. And when I declared this to God, along with my promise to give thanks every day for the life I was living, a darkness embraced me with warmth and comfort. I felt safe there, as if it were a womb of sorts. In the darkness, I wasn't alone, as music was also with me and took its place as the awakener in my journey.

My physical body was still in a coma, but my spiritual self needed a way to come back to embodiment. In the darkness I saw a colorful musical staff in the distance. The musical staff was alive with animated music notes and each note, each pitch, was a different color. I saw the music moving along the staff, playing an unheard melody. It moved steadily toward me, until it became bigger than my field of vision — and then the giant, moving, musical staff moved *right through me.*

Without a trace, it vanished, replaced by a tiny pinprick of light in a sea of darkness. My focus intensified on the light, and then I heard the faint sound of music. It was nearly inaudible; I had to channel all my energy to determine if it was even real. The sound and light were one. I focused intently on the music, which took great effort.

On Earth, I was still in the ICU of the hospital in Waco. It was day five of my coma. As suggested, my parents had been playing home movies and cartoons at my bedside to engage my mind. On this day, however, Dad decided to play the movie "Sleeping Beauty," an adaptation of an opera filled with classical music. Miraculously, even in my comatose state, the music from "Sleeping Beauty" resonated deeply with me. The melody was the guiding light that brought me me back to the realm of the living.

I can still remember how challenging it was to come back into my body. My sole focus was on bringing the sound of the music closer. I used every ounce of energy that I could muster to call in the music. As I pulled it closer, it began to occupy more of the space within me. It became louder and louder. Eventually the music was booming so loudly in my head that it became uncomfortable; I no longer doubted that the sound was real.

With every effort to make the music louder, I had been drawing myself closer. As the music reached an uncomfortably loud intensity, I could only think of one way to escape. I forced my eyes open.

When I opened my eyes, the music stopped abruptly, though the movie was still playing at my bedside. My senses were unstable. I could either see or hear, but not both. I saw the hospital curtain around the bed across from me, and noticed the movie credits scrolling up the screen of a television cart positioned to the right of my bed. As the nurse ran towards me, I slipped out of consciousness again.

So began my journey to recovery. It would take several years to heal my physical body, but during that time, my spiritual-self thrived. I had awakened to something greater than myself, returning with a purpose to use music for healing. Upon waking, I immersed myself in music, playing with passion and dedication. Music became my refuge, a pathway to physical and emotional healing following the head injury.

The wisdom I gained from the other side has shaped my life, guiding every choice I make. To this day, nothing is as real or loving as that experience. Because of this, when faced with a crossroads or choice in my life, everything circles back to that moment, and I ask myself:

"Does this experience reflect the light and love of Heaven?"

If it does not, I choose to let it go. But if it resonates with the same luminous energy, I embrace it wholeheartedly.

Now that you're acquainted with my story, I'm eager to guide you in accessing spiritual aspects of yourself. In this first exercise, I invite you to experience a meditation using music. This practice is designed to help you connect with the depths of your inner self, much like the journey of my NDE. Allow the harmonious melodies to guide you through a transformative exploration, tapping into your spiritual essence. May this meditation be a catalyst for unlocking the gifts within you and fostering a deeper connection to your inner being. May these gifts become guiding lights, leading you towards a life abundant with harmony, infinite joy, and boundless possibilities.

Meditation for Journeying to Heaven and Back

THE GOLDEN HEART SUN MEDITATION WITH MUSIC

1. Find Your Sacred Space: Begin by finding a peaceful space where you won't be disturbed. You may want to light a candle or diffuse oils to create a tranquil atmosphere.

2. Create an Intention: Reflect on your desired outcome. Write it down and begin to think about how its realization would change your life for the greatest good.

3. Choose Your Music: Now, choose a piece of instrumental music to accompany your meditation. Opt for music without words, pref-erably longer than four minutes. Classical music often works beautifully. Ensure you have it ready to play.

4. Breathe and Relax: Sit or lie down comfortably and close your eyes. Take a few deep breaths, inhaling through your nose and exhaling through your mouth. Feel any tension leaving your body with each exhale.

5. The Golden Heart Sun: Visualize a radiant golden sun at the center of your chest, your heart center. As you breathe in, imagine this golden sun getting brighter and more expansive.

6. Expanding Light: With each breath, see this golden sun growing larger, filling your entire chest with its warm, luminous light. As it expands, it touches every part of your being, illuminating your soul and warming your heart. See it expanding beyond your body, your room, the roof line, the cloud line, the atmosphere and the Earth.

7. Connect to Your Inner Presence: See your Higher Self in all its glory shining love down on you. See the perfection and beauty of this Presence and feel the unconditional love and acceptance. Feel a ray of light shining down on you, pouring the perfection of your Presence on and around you.

8. Begin Your Music: Play your music and continue to feel your Presence beaming down on you, showering you with light and love. Imagine what color this beam is, allowing your body to embody ev-ery quality of this cleansing, peaceful light.

You can find music suggestions and recordings of my medita-tions on my website at *www.wellnessmusictherapy.com.*

9. Deep Listening: As the instrumental music begins to play, let the music become the light washing over you. This music is the soundtrack to your inner journey. Feel the heat within your heart expand as you pull in more light and love.

10. Inner Exploration: With the music as your guide, visualize the positive manifestation of your intention. Visualize and feel what your life would be like if it were to be true. Ask yourself:

- Who would accompany me if this intention were realized?
- Where would I go? What would I be doing?
- How can I use this intention as a gift to bring healing and love to myself and others?
- What would my day-to-day life look like?
- How would it feel to be in the joy of this accomplishment?

11. Receiving through the Music: Allow the music to be a guiding force as you surrender to the emotions of joy that accompany the positive manifestation of your intention. Be open to any insights or messages that may arise during this meditation, and follow your visions. Let the music wash over you like a wave of joy.

12. Gratitude: When you feel ready, express gratitude for this experience and any insights you've received. Know that you can come back to these feelings at any time by simply recalling the images that came to you today.

13. Reflect and Journal: Take time to reflect on your experience while still in your mind. Consider keeping a journal to capture your thoughts, revelations, and ideas that emerged during this meditation.

You can find recordings of this meditation
on my website at ***www.wellnessmusictherapy.com***

CHAPTER 2

Unveiling the Hidden Path

We are electric light beings, tuned into powerful
frequencies — walking bundles of sound and light waves.
We play the universe's music through the
instruments of our existence.

I ENTERED a restful phase in the years following the accident, allowing time to provide the space to heal from my NDE. After all, there was much to integrate, and I was still a child. Being only twelve years old when I had my NDE, it took time for me to start sharing my story with others.

I saw interesting visions after awakening. For instance, I could see light around people and noticed quickly that some people had more light than others. I realized that people with more light around them were people I could trust and confide in. I also could see colors surrounding individuals, although their exact meaning eluded me. It wasn't until much later in my life, during my training in spirituality, that I gained a deeper understanding of the meaning behind these colors.

When I woke up, I believed everyone could see these lights and colors. I shared openly at first and found that not everyone understood me. My family supported me, but some friends started to see me as strange, and my worry about what they thought made me hide parts of myself. I stopped sharing messages and didn't talk about the light I saw around people. Instead, I focused on figuring out why I had these intuitive gifts. I didn't feel like I fit in, but I always kept my promise to God to be thankful. Each night, I expressed my gratitude, and that was the starting point for me to integrate my NDE into my life.

Growing Up:
Intuition, Spirituality, and Physical Healing

When I first woke from the coma, I had no memory of my life prior to my head injury. The doctors grimly told me that if I were to regain any memories, they'd arise in the first five years as my brain healed. After that critical period, they warned, my ability to remember life before my head injury would be gone forever. Despite facing this challenging prognosis and having deficits in cognitive abilities, I found that I was compensated for these shortcomings through the development of my spiritual gifts. Each step in my journey unlocked new skills, starting with synesthesia, the ability to see colors in sound and a phenomenon I call Harmonic Resonance, which is when I feel music resonating within different parts of my body.

For years, I waited for memories that never came. Only a handful of memories came to me in the first five years, but nothing of real substance. There were no memories of birthdays or first days of school. I couldn't remember the names of best friends or some of my family members. I didn't remember the dance recitals, family vacations, or swim meets. It was all blank. My mother painted the picture of a beautiful childhood, but as hard as I tried, I couldn't remember.

In the late 80s, there were not good rehabilitative services to support my neurological recovery. I navigated the world as best I could amidst all the after-effects of a head injury, including intense and ever-changing emotions, difficulty finding words, memory issues and debilitating headaches. Through it all, I stayed focused, knowing these were all recovery issues that would not last forever.

I learned to "fake it until I could make it," which gave me even greater lessons about humankind. After all, with my injured brain, I struggled to comprehend even half of what people discussed, often thinking they spoke too rapidly for me to grasp. I felt lost in conversations. My mom gave me the best tool when she told me to simply make eye contact, smile, and pretend that I knew what was going on. It turned out to be one of my best lessons in recovery and life.

It gave me the chance to practice another powerful lesson of my near-death experience: releasing the story. Why is letting go of our cognitive story important? Because, in the end, the story we create about ourselves and others *doesn't really matter.*

On the other side, the message was:

"Most of what we worry about in life doesn't matter. It's a distraction from our Presence. Love matters. People matter. How you live matters. The fears, the worries, the perceived transgressions... They are all distractions! We are here to lift each other up, surrender, trust, guide people out of fear and help them connect with their inner power and wisdom."

Perhaps this is why I came back with no memory. I had no story, so I had to learn to engage with the world on a spiritual level. With no personal history for me to remember, I forgot any and all issues that could anchor me in old patterns. This freedom allowed me to be completely open and trusting, not only with myself but also with others. I discovered the gift of detaching from the details as I tuned in to people's emotions and experiences. Whether they were happy or sad, I learned to connect with Source to hear and share the underlying spiritual messages that were coming to me. Through curiosity, compassion, and a deep connection fostered by my link to the other side, I became a student of the human experience.

By practicing detachment, I came to realize that what most people truly desired was a sense of belonging and understanding. People wanted to know they were accepted. They received my messages, which always seemed to serve as a reminder of their inner strength and wisdom.

As I got better at this, I started noticing that people's stories often had common themes related to spiritual ideas I learned from my near-death experience. As I shared spiritual messages, I didn't mention where they came from. People found these messages really helpful. They started to recognize their own power to shift their lives, which inspired me to practice this skill even more.

In 9TH grade, I remember a friend coming to me in tears after a fight with her mother. She felt her world was crumbling. She was lost in the despair and emotion of her pain. I listened and asked questions to help her move through the issue. I asked her if there was a greater lesson to her trauma, and we went on to discuss how these types of experiences are an opportunity to choose a new response. Could she learn to respond in love?

At that moment, I shared a message from Source with her, telling her she would have a future in healing others and that it would start with her own healing journey. She realized that she was meant to heal her family through experience. Her grandmother came through and as I helped her connect with her grandmother's presence, she saw the light surrounding herself and felt the loving energy.

With a deep exhale, it all clicked into place. She understood that she was a healer, and everything happening in her life was guiding her to discover this part of herself. Her life changed from that point onward. She saw the purpose in her pain and began to embrace her role as a healer, bringing healing to her family. Later in life, she even learned to work with healing ancestral lines.

My emerging intuitive gifts gave me something, as well. They helped me make friends quickly. I'd found a way to feel as though I belonged. I shared spiritual messages without revealing their divine origin, which allowed me to share my gifts without the fear of being perceived as peculiar or exposed. I was living in the joy of the light and I'd found a way to bring it to others! It brought comfort to my adolescent self, knowing that I was accepted, and taught me that I could connect with others, even while dealing with ongoing cognitive challenges of my NDE.

As I continued my physical healing, I just wanted to be "normal." I developed tools and tricks that helped me cope with the world and avoid the frustration of being confused all the time. Besides pretending that I understood things and simply learning to smile when I didn't know what to do, I learned to joke as a deflection for my lack of understanding. I found it was easier to plead ignorance than to explain my cognitive difficulties. It made life easier.

I never did recover many memories but that didn't matter much because I was so thankful to be alive. I think back about how heartbreaking it must have been for my parents when they reminded me of an amazing vacation, memory, or childhood accomplishment, only to hear me reply: "Oh, I don't remember that." So, I continued hiding my experience and pretending I understood things. I learned to act like I knew what I was doing until it became real.

I could also sense others' disbelief when I shared my NDE with them. It's like they wanted to believe it, but it was so far from their experience that they couldn't entertain the possibility that there is more out there. I often wondered why some people preferred to think I was making things up rather than considering the idea of a real Divine Presence.

I told myself that my story was not ready to be shared. Source messages were coming to me continually, but I still needed to learn how to truly receive them. At that point I had not learned to maintain boundaries, making me too much of an open channel for the spiritual and emotional energy of others. I stepped back a bit, only sharing messages with friends who were willing to hear them.

I lived my life through music. It became my healing tool, my way to escape, and a means to express my creativity. I never forgot my mission to heal through music, but I knew I had to heal myself first. Healing through music meant that it became an extension of myself. This is when I discovered the gift of synesthesia.

When I played my flute or music on the piano, I became an emotional and spiritual conduit of energy. Time stopped, all pain or fear left my body, and I was once again reunited with the realm of love and light. I became dedicated to my art, practicing all the time and using my musical abilities to help me find my identity and place in the world. I started seeing colors from the music. What a magical world it was!

Seeing colors through music, known as synesthesia, is a spiritual gift where the stimulation of one sensory pathway, like hearing music, leads to involuntary experiences in another pathway, such as seeing colors. It's a unique and subjective way of perceiving the world, blending sensory experiences in a distinct manner.

I watched the colors of music through my mind's eye, and my delight deepened as another gift came forward. I call it Harmonic Resonance, and I've been seeking others who share this experience. I will do my best to describe it.

As I play music, I can feel the music coursing through me, resonating within my bones. Each note has a unique placement, creating a symphony of sensations in different areas of my back, neck, and head. When playing in a symphony or band setting, each instrument contributed a distinct body sensation. The drums pulsated in my head, stringed instruments played melodies along my spine, violins gracefully moved along the upper spine, while lower stringed instruments such as the cello resonated in my lower back and tailbone. This is Harmonic Resonance.

Through the magic of music, I found a daily portal to reconnect with Heaven, a transcendent feeling that envelops my entire being. I wonder if this experience came with me from the other side or if it developed as a new way of communication when I closed off my intuitive channels. Either way, it is clear that music had become the language through which Source communicated with me.

Fueled by my deep connection to music and all that it had brought into my life, I held to my commitment to someday heal people through music, although I didn't possess a clear roadmap for how that would happen. I placed my trust in the universe, believing that it would provide a path when the time was right.

In the meantime, I continued my daily ritual to express gratitude for the precious gift of life and embraced every experience, regardless of how challenging it might be. I learned to uncover seeds of gratitude even amidst my most challenging moments. I expressed thanks for the lessons learned in teenage moments with friends and the challenges I faced in my classes. I even found gratitude my physical limitations and the headaches resulting from my head injury. Each experience served as a reminder that I was *alive*, and that in itself was enough. Even at a young age, I knew that creating my Heaven on Earth would start by embracing gratitude *as much as possible*. This ongoing practice became an integral part of my reality, a constant reminder of my vow to God and a reinforcement of a future when I would learn to heal others through the transformative power of music.

Cultivating Spiritual Gifts:
Gratitude and Games with Friends

Gratitude wasn't always easy. During my teens, I'd get debilitating headaches that made me nauseous. I called them "horse headaches." The doctors prescribed high dosages of ibuprofen. The headaches got increasingly better in the second, third and fourth year, downgrading to more typical headaches, and eventually leaving altogether.

It was those first few years when I began to relearn things that I'd forgotten. I sat in front of VHS home movies for hours, watching myself blowing out birthday candles, all while wishing I could recall the names of those who had joined my celebrations. I struggled with jumbled words and rearranged phrases, which was very amusing to my brothers. They laughed when I asked for "acon and beggs" for breakfast or described life as "going uphill without a paddle."

These moments brought fun and joy to my recovery and allowed me to keep my sense of humor. Humor became a healing tool for me. After my parents mentioned it a few times, I'd jokingly call myself a miracle. Why should I get to ride in the front seat? Because I'm a miracle, of course!

I kept my NDE sacred, sharing only with those I trusted. Most people wanted to fit my story into what they knew of NDEs, which took away from the experience for me. My story wasn't the typical tunnel with the white light at the end, which people expected to hear. However, I knew in my heart that what I had experienced was real and powerful. I was so committed to preserving the authenticity of my experience that I even avoided reading about other NDE accounts, fearing that it might diminish what I had gone through.

Opportunities to integrate my NDE came through friendships that acted as life teachers, and this continues to this day. Teachers have a way of showing up in our lives in beautiful and unexpected ways. The next part of this book is designed to guide you in cultivating similar friendships to deepen your spiritual gifts. One of my first great teachers during this time was my best friend, Kathleen. We loved sharing the synchronicities of the universe with each other. I'd tell her about the messages that I received and we would delight when we found them to be true. We made a game of sharing signs of validation with each other and would find ways to relate them to our lives. It was like a treasure hunt for hidden meanings and connections every day. By discussing them openly, we learned to trust our intuitive abilities even more.

The signs came in many ways: lyrics to a song that came on at the perfect time, symbols in nature, dreams, or visions. We noticed every little thing. This "noticing" practice brought us joy and helped us see how consistently Source is communicating with us. When we found validating signs in the world, Source rewarded us by giving us even more.

The game we had playfully devised was, in fact, a means of training ourselves to enhance our intuitive abilities. As we received signs and checked them with each other, we were honing our intuitive gifts, gradually cultivating a heightened sense of discernment. During this time, I learned to distinguish between messages from a higher source and those that were just products of my thoughts or imagination. Emotionless dreams often carried spiritual significance, while emotionally charged ones were almost always related to working through issues in my personal life. This skill proved valuable in guiding myself and others on their spiritual journeys.

This game of developing intuition worked. In my teens and early twenties, more lessons propelled me forward on my spiritual path, developing practical skills I would later need.

I became very active in my church, finding inspiration in sermons and other reminders of our connection to God. I became fascinated in all things spiritual. More and more, I would "know" things before they happened. My dreams became more prophetic and I also started seeing more colors and light around my friends.

These budding intuitive skills arrived just in time for me to embark on my educational journey. By the time I was ready to step into my Masters program, I'd found a spiritually-based school that seemed to possess a magical quality. Everything was leading me where I needed to go. Within the transformative halls of Naropa University, my spiritual connection was refined. I found myself in the company of others who shared aspirations of unlocking their divine spiritual potential and navigating their own unique path.

Bridging Education with My Near-Death Experience

I had a deep conviction that the universe would provide me with the way to integrate my NDE into my future work but had no idea what that would look like. Luckily during my early twenties, I discovered music therapy, which seemed to hold the key.

Following my father's recommendation, I pursued a dual master's degree in music therapy and psychology, with only two universities offering this unique program. I chose Naropa University in Boulder, Colorado, for its distinctive approach blending contemplative practices like meditation with psychology training. Guided by the knowledge that the universe had a plan for me, I always knew my "why," and Naropa provided me with the "how."

Naropa is referred to as the "Hogwarts of the real world" by some of its graduates. Those who have completed its programs know it to be a transformative experience in its own right. As a student of Transpersonal Psychology with an emphasis in Music Therapy, I was pushed to my spiritual limits and beyond. The program challenged me to explore the boundaries of spiritual expansion while also being immersed in the therapeutic process.

Although there were eight other students initially enrolled in the music therapy program, financial aid issues forced seven to drop out and the eighth had to leave due to personal circumstances during the second week. As a result, I became the sole music therapy student in my year. This allowed me to dive deeply into the study of altered states of consciousness, with a focus on the use of music and imagery. My program became a private study, providing me with a unique and personalized education.

During my time at Naropa University, a moment of true synchronicity occurred for me in the first week of classes. As I climbed the stairs to my meditation class on Arapahoe Avenue, I saw a painting of Buddha hanging on the wall. He was depicted as thin and bald, with brown robes, and appeared younger than other renderings I had seen. Instantly I recognized him as the guide who had stood to my left on the raft during my near-death experience. This painting served as a validation, affirming that Naropa was the right choice.

Over the next few years, I practiced meditation and learned the value of being fully present in the moment. A few months into my meditation practice, I started seeing vivid colors around people as they meditated in the meditation hall. Each person radiated their own unique color, creating a stunning display.

This phenomenon came only when I was fully present, presumably when I was most in tune with my energetic body. I had to release expectations to tap into this state of being. Each day I practiced releasing expectation and sinking more and more into awareness of the present moment until it became easier. I knew I had achieved this state of complete presence when I felt what I call the "whoosh," inspired by the surges of energy that hit the top of my head when I fully call in my higher presence.

During these experiences, there is a sense of lightness and warmth that floods the area behind my closed eyes. I often feel a rush of warm, loving energy moving in through the top of my head as I exhale.

You can try this for yourself by closing your eyes, allowing your outer body to be still, and being present in the moment. Close your eyes and turn them upward to look at your third eye, the center point between the eyebrows. Then sit for a moment, releasing all thoughts as they come. Allow the outbreath to be a reminder to release anything that no longer serves you. Perhaps even hold your closed-eye gaze looking at the back of your third eye. Over time, you will learn to call in this energy as you need it, as well as learning to stay in this energy for longer periods of time.

At Naropa, I discovered the intriguing world of altered states of consciousness and acquired the skills to guide others on journeys into the spiritual realm. This education marked the inception of the approach that defines my work. Ultimately, my work centers around helping others in establishing a connection with their higher presence, so they can receive their own messages from beyond.

I discovered in my training that altered states of consciousness offer access to different brainwave states that allow us to transcend the stories that trap us in the human experience. Instead, we can directly address and clear the emotions underlying these narratives, granting us direct access to a higher power. I learned to escape the narrative by guiding clients through music programs and guided imagery, channeling messages from the angelic realm. This skill allowed me to bridge the intuitive gifts originating in my NDE and assist clients in connecting with messages from beyond.

The program's emphasis on Transpersonal Psychology provided me with a unique perspective on the human experience, and the music and imagery techniques I learned have played a pivotal role in my career as a spiritual coach and music therapist.

Here's a tool that I've found helpful in my own journey

of self-discovery. "Releasing to Inner Presence" is designed to help you let go of the need for immediate answers about your life's purpose. Instead, it encourages you to trust in your inner Presence to guide you along your unique path. Through this exercise, I invite you to step out of the thinking mind, fostering a direct connection with Source. It serves as a practice to invoke the fullness of energy, allowing you to call it in and experience its presence.

Releasing to Higher Presence Meditation

1. Preparation: Find a quiet and comfortable space. Sit with your back straight and your hands resting on your lap, palms facing up.

2. Relaxation: Close your eyes and take a few deep breaths. Inhale deeply through your nose, hold for a moment, and exhale slowly through your mouth.

3. Setting Intentions: Set a clear intention such as "I want to understand my life's purpose through the lens of my higher presence."

4. Reflect and Ask: Ask yourself the following questions:
- "What brings me joy and fulfillment?"
- "What am I passionate about?"
- "What are my unique talents and abilities?"

5. Release to Higher Presence: Imagine these questions as butterflies in your hand. Visualize yourself letting go of these butterflies, allowing them to float up into the sky. As they ascend, release attachment to the answers and feel lightness as they move further and further from you.

6. Affirmation: Repeat a positive affirmation to yourself. "I trust in my Presence to guide me to my life's purpose in perfect timing."

7. Gratitude: Express gratitude for this moment of release and trust in your Presence.

8. Closing: Slowly return to your awareness of the present moment. Open your eyes when you're ready.

This meditation helps you release the need to have immediate answers about your life's purpose, trusting that your Presence will guide your journey of self-discovery.

CHAPTER 3

Journey to Authenticity

When we embrace the consciousness within
every plant, every animal, each experience, every object,
and every relationship, we are acknowledging the meaningful
threads woven through our engagement with this planet.
It is then that we realize we are free.

I GOT MARRIED and started a family soon after completing my master's degree. I was in my mid-twenties at the time. I had met my husband in high school in my teens and dated him through college and graduate school. I worked for about a year before getting pregnant with our first child. Then I stayed at home with my children and embraced the gift of motherhood.

During that time, I was grateful to be able to stay home with my children. I relished in the small, but meaningful joys of motherhood — from baking birthday cakes and making cute Pinterest-based snacks, to hosting playdates and singing songs with them. I also tended to their educational and therapeutic needs and loved every minute of it. Though it wasn't always easy, I cherished the opportunity to watch my children grow and explore the world around them. Being a mother is my greatest gift, and I am forever grateful for that time with them.

Despite all that, I still felt like I was hiding, and it wasn't just because I was focused on motherhood. There were underlying issues in my marriage that made me feel like I couldn't be fully myself. I tried to be the best mother I could be, but I also felt like I had to suppress parts of myself that didn't fit my husband's mold of the perfect wife and mother.

I was compartmentalizing my spiritual side for the sake of our family. The decision to hide was born of my own fear of judgment and abandonment.

I realize now that this is a common struggle for many, especially those who have felt pressured or conditioned to prioritize others before themselves. We can feel out of touch with our spiritual side, our passions, and our purpose, as we slip into the roles we believe we are supposed to be playing or try to be the people that others expect us to be. Sometimes we hide to protect ourselves or our families, but in doing so, we also hide our gifts, our talents, and our true selves. This self-imposed hiding can create a prison of confusion and inauthenticity, leaving us to wonder if there is more to life than what we've settled for.

Hiding the authentic self resonates deeply with many healers. Throughout history, those with extraordinary healing powers and gifts have often been doubted, ridiculed, or even persecuted. A mix of fear and cultural conditioning has led many of us to operate from the shadows and only share our gifts when it feels safe. I grappled with the intense fear of judgment, which arose from a strong need for safety in my world. Giving in to this fear led to self-imposed limitations and a feeling of inauthenticity. This is exactly where I found myself within my marriage.

Combining my fear of judgment with my partner's own fears and need for control, I felt increasingly alone and disconnected. My fears prevented me from fully expressing myself to him, thereby deepening my tendency to hide my true self.

As I continued to evolve and grow in my late thirties, I began to recognize my own worthiness and shed the cloak of invisibility that I had placed on myself. I began to see opportunities to share my NDE and found support from those who were willing to listen. It was liberating to finally recognize my value. I shared my story while working with the healing powers of frequencies, oils, and sound. I found joy in helping others on their own spiritual journeys. Even with the demands of motherhood, I carved out time when the kids were in school to embrace the juicy spiritual space that brought me so much fulfillment.

The time for hiding was over. I felt a drive to step into something greater. Looking back, I see that each small step I took was guiding me to break free from the shackles of spiritual oppression. I began attracting like-minded people into my life, which marked the beginning of another layer of awakening, and the magic that followed was beyond my wildest dreams.

As I reflect on that period of my life, I see that I needed that time to fully integrate my experiences. Through dedicated inner work, I brought this newfound knowledge into my daily life. Each step of the way I was rewarded with some type of magical experience.

Countless lessons have come between then and now, but one experience stands out as particularly significant. During a sound journey circle I held for a friend, everyone laid down with closed eyes and called in messages of support and love as I played the crystal singing bowls. I noticed that one friend, Jeanine, wasn't lying down with the others. She was sitting up and watching me as I facilitated the circle. In the moment, I worried this was a sign that she was not enjoying the process. However, I made a conscious effort to release these thoughts and remain present to facilitating the experience. After the circle, Jeanine approached me and asked, "Do you know how you are receiving messages?"

I responded, "Not really, they just come."

She then explained, "When you play the bowls, a large female angel is with you. She loves the crystal singing bowls and comes through to support your work. When you share angel messages at the end of the session, you are connecting directly with your own Higher Presence for those messages. I haven't seen that before."

I was intrigued. I wanted to know more about Jeanine and

her work. I felt so seen by her and felt a strong sense of alignment. I knew instantly that I was meant to work with her.

Jeanine and I decided to do a session trade. I gave her a
music, imagery and angel reading session. In return, she took
a photo of my aura and led me through an energy reading
and healing. When we reviewed the photo of my aura, it revealed a surprising split in the middle of my body, with two
distinct colors — fuchsia on one side, and green on the other.
Initially, Jeanine thought that she needed to fix my aura, but
upon further reflection, she realized that it was how I hold
energy and there was nothing to "fix." She explained that
held both divine masculine and feminine energies within me,
and that it was crucial for me to integrate and access both of
these energies in my personal and professional life.

She also described two light beings that were with me, a
large female angelic being, and a small, short unicorn.

The fact that she saw a tiny unicorn both delighted and
intrigued me. You see, I've always had a deep connection to
unicorns and have turned to them for healing and support
since childhood. When Jeanine mentioned that the unicorn's
name was Uni, I was astounded. She had no way of knowing,
but I had a childhood stuffed animal with the same name, and
my parents told me I used to sleep with it every night. After
my head injury, I'd visualize a unicorn in my mind's eye, especially during stressful times, imagining myself lying on its
belly in a lush green field, releasing all my fears. She had intuitively accessed my spirit animal!

The fact that Jeanine knew the name of my spirit animal without me mentioning it was remarkable. No one but my family knew that. This reinforced the idea that there is a deep connection between the spiritual and physical realms.

Jeanine also revealed that I had left a portion of my soul body on the other side during my NDE and that it was meant to be reunited with me at the right time, which was during that session. She continued her balancing techniques using oils, crystals, and by connecting to Source. During the session, she had a vision of a "cosmic egg" moving into my physical body. As she shared this with me, I experienced strong currents of energy pulsing down my right side and then again on the left side, until all the energy rushed to a spot just above my head and remained there. The sensation was powerful, and I felt complete.

I had my session with Jeanine in 2018 — 29 years after my head injury. It took that long for me to heal and call back the part of my soul that was left on the other side. During our meeting, Jeanine predicted that because I reconnected to the missing part of my higher presence during the session with her, there would be significant changes in my life over the next year.

Her prediction was right. Things started falling into place and aligning just as she had foreseen. Within months of our meeting, my life and marriage underwent a complete shift, and I found myself on a path that I could never have imagined. This experience taught me that integration is a gradual process, and that it takes time and life experience to bring all the pieces of our journey together.

In recent years, as I've found the courage to share my NDE more openly, I'm consistently reminded that we're all in this together. Each person we meet is another piece to the puzzle. A gift presented for us to rediscover some hidden piece of knowledge or part of ourselves. Through Jeanine, the universe had given me magical signs of validation, reaffirming my belief that we're always connected to something greater than ourselves. I believe now, more than ever before, that it's time for all of us to step into this connection, to embrace our innate spirituality and to celebrate the unique gifts that each of us brings to the world.

As you explore and strengthen your connection to your own Presence, the following exercise will help you acknowledge the people in your life who have served as guides. This exercise will encourage reflection on how life has led you to this point. By acknowledging the guidance around you, you can also use this exercise to open doors to deeper spiritual connections and a greater understanding of your unique role in our planetary awakening.

✳ ✳ ✳

Life Reflection Journaling Exercise

I. Life Reflection and Purpose Recognition
- Set aside time to journal about significant moments and experiences in your life that have shaped who you are today.
- Consider how these events have contributed to your personal growth and understanding.

- Recognize patterns or themes that may reveal aspects of your unique path and purpose.
- Contemplate how your life's journey has led you to this moment and the possibilities that lie ahead.

II. Acknowledging Guiding Relationships

- Take a moment to think about individuals in your life who have played a guiding role or have inspired and supported you on your journey.
- Write down their names and reflect on the positive impact they've had.
- Express gratitude for these relationships, whether through a written note, a mental acknowledgment, or in a conversation with them.

III. Self-Forgiveness Meditation

- Prepare Your Space: Find a quiet and comfortable space. Close your eyes and take deep breaths to center yourself.
- Reflect on Self-Judgment: Identify areas of guilt or self-judgment. Allow these emotions to surface without judgment.
- Practice Self-Forgiveness: Acknowledge your humanity and deserve compassion. Visualize releasing burdens, creating space for self-love.

- Incorporate Ho'oponopono Prayer*
  1. *"I'm sorry"* — Reflect on actions causing pain. Say *"I'm sorry"* to yourself.
  2. *"Please forgive me"* — Extend forgiveness for past mistakes.
  3. *"Thank you"* — Express gratitude for lessons and growth.
  4. *"I love you"* — Cultivate self-love and compassion.

Close the Meditation

Take a moment of silence to let its meaning sink in. Conclude your journaling session by imagining a future filled with self-forgiveness, gratitude, and love. Visualize how these qualities can shape your journey ahead. Close your journal and take a few more deep breaths. Carry the sense of self forgiveness, gratitude, and love with you as you continue your life's journey. Concentrate on positive language, feeling and visualization practices as you do this.

Explanation of the Ho'oponopono Prayer:

The Ho'oponopono prayer is an ancient Hawaiian practice of reconciliation and forgiveness. It consists of four simple phrases: *"I'm sorry, please forgive me, thank you, I love you."* This prayer is not only a means of seeking forgiveness and reconciliation with others but also a tool for healing and self-forgiveness.

CHAPTER 4

Spiritual Initiation

In seeking enlightenment, we discover the golden light
beneath the darkness — the dark night of the soul,
a crucial step for spiritual evolution.

SOURCE can bring us necessary lessons by pulling the rug out from under us. When we lose connection to ourselves by becoming too immersed in something that isn't aligned with our true purpose, an experience may come along to shake us up. This ego-death is an opportunity to confront our deepest vulnerabilities and make a choice between embracing love or fear.

Jack Canfield, a motivational speaker and author, has been a major influence in my life and work. He shares the concept of love versus fear in his book titled *The Success Principles: How to Get from Where You Are to Where You Want to Be*. This concept is discussed in the context of personal development and achieving success in various aspects of life. In line with Jack's perspective, this process of dis-identifying from our ego grants us the chance for a rebirth of our true selves.

Our lives may look like they are being turned upside down

at times, but in reality, what if we are actually being redirected so we can get back on track, spiritually? This process is
known by various names in different wisdom traditions, with
one commonly referenced term being "The Dark Night of the
Soul." My dark night of the soul began in my early forties when
my marriage of twenty years dissolved.

Upon reflection, it is clear that deep down, I knew that
my ex-husband wasn't meant to be my lifelong partner. Nev-
ertheless, our coming together served a purpose, and despite
enduring challenging lessons through our relationship, he
played a pivotal role as a teacher in my life. He also gave me
the blessing of my beautiful children.

Early in our marriage, he had become dismissive of my
gifts, disinterested in my spiritual journey, rarely asking me to
share more about that part of my life. This felt strange because
he seemed initially drawn to me because of my NDE. My experience was of the light, while his NDE story was surrounded by fear and darkness.

We shared our NDEs when we first met through mutual
friends in high school. We also shared a passion for music.
Initially, he listened to my NDE with fascination, asking questions about what I learned on the other side. He was mesmerized by my experience and seemed to gain hope from it. It
was drastically different from his feeling of leaving his body to
find uncertainty and darkness. Back then, he enjoyed hearing
me play music and spoke often of my gifts. I felt safe sharing
more intimately with him because of his admiration of my

musical talents.

However, when he became skeptical and dismissive it felt safer to go silent, immersing myself in building a life for our kids, rather than expressing myself fully. My spiritual path revealed itself to me through motherhood. Source never leaves us and always has a plan.

My children, whom I always knew would bring a special energy to the world, served as another of my most significant teachers. Through mother's intuition, reading their cries and changing expressions, I developed a deeper understanding of their unspoken needs and emotions, honing my intuitive skills much like I had directly after my NDE. I felt connected to them in a way that felt like an extension of my own being.

In early motherhood there were times when sleep eluded me, and I would lie awake wondering why. Inevitably a baby's cry or a little one seeking comfort after a nightmare would fill the silence. It dawned on me that my intuition was directing me to stay awake so I could help when they needed me the most. Over time, I honed this skill, tuning in earlier and earlier each evening. As I got better, I found that by six or seven p.m., I could sense if I needed to stay up later to be available for them in the later evening and plan my night accordingly. In aligning with their needs, I was developing my predictive intuition.

Being a mother became my spiritual practice, in which I found joy and love in every moment. Despite my own struggles and uncertainties, I knew that I was still being led by

Source, and I continued to give thanks every day for my life. In this way, motherhood helped me step more fully into my spiritual gifts and embrace my true purpose in life.

I started seeing spiritual visions when I was nursing my children. Once, when I was nursing my youngest, my great uncle, Buddy came to me. He was wearing a green Army service uniform and a hat, and was smiling ear to ear. He stood there silently in quiet, peaceful energy. I knew at once that he was saying goodbye. I found out later that he'd gone into a coma that day and died soon after. I felt honored that he'd come to me. Years later, the night that his wife passed away, the two of them came to me, happy to be together again. Showing me that they had made it into the light.

As I cared for my children, I also started teaching them to develop their own intuition. Each night, I would have quiet conversations with them before bed, playing music and singing to them, helping them to release their fears into the light. We talked about the magic of sleep, and imagined a powerful animal protecting us as we rested. I taught them about the invisible string that connected our hearts, and we discussed where we went when we slept. I also told them to imagine being surrounded by a protective bubble, and I blessed them with my own form of protection. In doing so, I wasn't just taking care of them as a mother; I was also learning how to teach others how to develop intuition.

The deeper I ventured into motherhood, the more I found myself confronting the disparities in parenting style between myself and my husband, which eventually shed light on all the issues between us. Early motherhood brought new forms of pressure, with society suggesting we adhere to certain parenting norms. Despite my attempts to conform, I preferred a gentler, holistic and education-based approach, while my husband insisted on stricter methods.

These differing approaches began to strain our relationship. As the children aged, he began inserting himself between me and our children, undermining my authority and even sending me away when they were upset. I remember our eight-year-old son crying as I stood at the threshold of his bedroom door wanting me to comfort him. I felt my husband was being too hard on him. He was beside himself and I just wanted to comfort him. My husband refused to let me even come into the room, telling me I needed to "go get a cup of coffee." I felt so helpless, knowing he thought I was too lenient. He blocked the door and sent me away. It was a challenging experience that demonstrated how different we were, not just in our parenting styles.

I was far from being a perfect parent and admittedly leaned towards being gentle. Through it all, my primary focus remained on parenting our children with love and compassion. They remain my greatest treasure, and the lessons I learn as a mother continue to shape my spiritual journey today.

To cope, I did my best to soak up the beautiful moments of motherhood and used that time to connect with Source. I am so thankful for that time and the support of the community

I met as a result. It was a valuable time in my life, even though my connection with God was private and the pace of messages of the Universe had slowed down.

I began re-engaging with my music therapy training by organizing monthly workshops. However, my husband convinced me that my work wasn't worth the cost of childcare. As the kids got older and more involved in school, I resolved that issue by working a bit during school hours.

I saw clients once a week and started using essential oils to support my health. At that time, I discovered I had chronic Lyme Disease, and was using any and all tools that I could to support my physical and mental health. I started receiving validation from Source that I was on the right path. I put oils on my skin, and noticed that my clients went deeper into the imagery process when they also applied oils. Through my work with clients, new spiritual gifts manifested once again, signaling I was raising my frequency.

One week, as part of my practice, I put Angelica oil on my hands to call in the angels before meeting with a client who we will call Jules. I did it for myself, because I found that I could see light beings more easily when I used that particular oil. Interestingly, my clients also reported seeing light beings when I used Angelica, despite not informing them beforehand. With ten out of eleven clients reporting the presence of angels in their imagery during the initial week of trying it, I decided I'd use Angelica oil before all my sessions.

In this session, Jules was lying with her eyes closed in a

deeply relaxed state. She started talking about hundreds of tiny light angels floating above her in her mind's eye. I looked up and saw light reflections in the shape of angels on the ceiling. There were hundreds of them! Her eyes were closed, so she couldn't see it, but saw it in her vision. I had never seen it before, and never saw it again. I investigated the room after the session, but never found where they were coming from. It was as if an invisible prism had blessed our sacred space.

Through my work, my purpose was returning to me. The light never left me, but was operating in its own time. As a mentor once told me: *"Everything happens on time, ahead of time, at the perfect time, and in divine order."*

And as if according to plan, a positive upward cycle developed. As I used oils, I was called to meditate more. As I meditated, I received an increasing number of messages from Source. I finally gave myself permission to share messages with colleagues and friends.

It started with the oils. Everyone loved them. They were little, high-vibe bottles of plant essence that raised my frequency, and they brought community. I found myself surrounded by high vibe, like-minded people. We shared stories of our successes with plant healing and connected daily to share what we'd learned. Whether it was helping with toddler meltdowns or providing support for better sleep, I bore witness to remarkable transformations occurring in the homes of those I cared for and admired, all thanks to the power of essential oils.

I see now that he oils were a gift to lift me through the next major phase of my life. *Everything was on time, ahead of time, at the perfect time, and in Divine order.*

I became very curious as to how these oils were helping everyone so much on an emotional level. I wondered why I'd never heard of them before. I started to dive into the research so much that I became fascinated. Others needed to know this information. It was life-changing. I was driven to teach others about them. The desire to teach inspired me to envision holding classes in my home.

Empowering Change:
Finding My Voice Amid Marital Stress

At first, my husband didn't support my idea to teach classes because he said we didn't have the money to hire a babysitter. I know now that we could have more than afforded childcare. It was just an excuse. His resistance was my first clue that something wasn't right. I became increasingly aware of how undervalued I was within the marriage.

My husband's resistance to my pursuits and the gradual realization of being undervalued created mounting tension. As I became more aware of this imbalance, the strain intensified, reaching a critical point one day just after my husband's grandmother passed away.

I'd known her and loved her from the time I was eighteen, which was longer than the thirteen years I'd known my own grandmother. The loss of his grandmother held significance for me, as she was a kind and loving person. However, its importance extended beyond grief, as the way he handled it showed me how he had regarded me within our marriage.

For her funeral, he was flying in from a business trip in England to a college town in central Indiana. Our daughter was flying from Colorado, where she was visiting my family. I was to travel from San Diego with my thirteen-year-old son and eight-year-old daughter. I wanted to fly to the airport closest to the funeral, so I wouldn't have to drive two hours from Cincinnati in the middle of the night with the kids. I remember thinking that if the price was right, it was a no-brainer to purchase tickets to the closer airport.

When I was ready to purchase the tickets, he refused to pay the thirty dollars required for each of our three tickets to be closer. I tried explaining the difficulty of traveling alone with the kids at midnight, but he wouldn't listen. His mother overheard our discussion and pleaded on our behalf, saying that it would be much better in the end for me and the children if I flew into the closer airport. She even offered to pay the difference.

He stopped her: "Don't spend your money on her, mom. We don't need your money. She doesn't need that."

It became evident that he didn't mind the challenges I faced. It was all about the bottom line. I ended up driving with the kids for two hours at midnight, arriving at the hotel at two a.m. on the funeral day, carefully bringing the kids quietly into the dark hotel room so as not to wake him up. Looking back,

I should have seen the warning signs, but it didn't take much longer to discover that he had, for a significant period, been prioritizing his own well-being over our well-being.

During this time, my husband had slipped into great insecurities around money. His money fears increasingly infringed on our lives. I was willing to accommodate his strange requests when I believed we were making changes that were for the good of the family. He used money for control and he was contributing only a portion of his paycheck to our family account. He even created secret accounts to hide money. His requests became increasingly controlling, and toward the end of our relationship, I found myself having to ask permission for any expenditure exceeding $50.

I was buying gas one day before school pickup, and the total was close to $50. When I arrived at the school after that, I decided to buy two pumpkins as part of the school fundraising project. The kids were so excited about those pumpkins! They'd helped to grow them with their classmates. Knowing the pumpkins would put me over my spending limit, I bought them, anyway.

When my husband found out that I'd spent over his maximum allowance, that's all he spoke of for days. I remember being so distraught and upset, crying all weekend because he said that I'd let the family down, I'd lost control of spending. I felt ashamed. The angst and tears over buying those two pumpkins was extreme, which completely took all the joy out of the experience.

He became so fearful about money that he used various tactics to build his individual wealth at the expense of our family. He was tucking a large part of his paycheck away while placing extreme limitations on me. Little by little, my freedoms felt stripped away. A stark absence of love, respect, and kindness permeated my life.

At this time, the children were getting older and needed medical care that was outside of the budget. I didn't know then that only a portion of his paycheck was making it into our account; I only knew that we needed money for healthcare and survival in the Southern California economy. I worked harder on my essential oils business (in secret) and began putting some food and medical expenses on a new credit card to pay off later. The expenses were adding up and I felt guilty about it. I didn't tell him about the card because of the shame I felt around money.

The truth always comes out, though. When it did, that was the nail in the coffin for us. That credit card seemed to anchor all his fears around money. He started to believe I was hiding other money from him, so we went to couples therapy to work on trust issues. I wasn't hiding money, but he didn't believe it until we divorced and he saw it for himself. His fears had a tangible impact on the energetic dynamics surrounding money.

Working with Jack Canfield in the aftermath of my divorce, and diving into his teachings on manifestation, brought clarity to the importance of my energetic connection to money.

The pieces of the puzzle seamlessly fit together as I co-facilitated Jack's Abundance Experience. It became evident that, within the confines of my marriage, the pursuit of a life filled with abundance was unattainable due to my ex-husband's perception of me and the fear he harbored around money.

In the end, I realized I needed to shift my own relationship with abundance by moving out from under the fears and limiting beliefs that had become such a prevalent part of my life and marriage. It was time to reclaim my power.

Looking back, it's evident that the way my marriage was destined for failure. Unreasonable expectations were set, impossible for anyone to meet. He projected his deceitful behaviors onto me. The mistake was letting him convince me that I was the problem. I stopped standing up for myself until I became a mere shadow of who I truly was.

Some might say I'd stepped into the role of the good wife, hiding everything that made me *me*. I felt trapped in a world of financial and emotional abuse, but I hid it willingly because I thought I was serving my family. In a sense, I was actively participating in my own devaluation. I think now that I even hid it from myself.

I made every effort to improve the situation, convinced that the fault lay with me. At least, that's what he told me. He once suggested that if I could anticipate his needs, everything would be fine. Would you believe I started trying to predict every issue he might face so I could address it in advance? When driving I searched for parking, planned the route, kept the kids content with snacks and games, played enjoyable music, and initiated entertaining conversations. When at home, I made sure the house was calm, meticulously tending to the kids to avert any potential meltdowns that would upset my husband. However, it proved to be an uphill battle. No matter how much I did, it was never enough. The root of the unhappiness lay within him, and I was merely the focal point of attention.

I was like a horse with blinders on, all while walking on eggshells around this man. I compartmentalized my spiritual self and learned to recognize his triggers and ignore my qualms about his personality.

I was mentally, physically and spiritually exhausted; I had a grayness to my coloring, and my light continued to fade. Whether he did this knowingly or unknowingly, it was his way to ensure he would have every reason to be dissatisfied.

Pictures show this gray energy that was around me. The only times I could feel or see the light around me and others was when I was using the oils, sharing tips with my community, alone with my kids, leading a music and imagery journey or playing my crystal singing bowls. The light came back to me in these moments. I remember a day when my friend Gina captured it on camera. She took pictures of me playing my crystal bowls and captured wings of light just behind me. Gina was thrilled to capture this on camera, and it was delightful to witness my light wings through the lens of her camera! Her deep appreciation for my work always humbled me.

The light revisits us when we engage in what we love and

what we are meant to do. So, just as the music was the hero in my awakening from the coma, it once again became my hero in reclaiming my life. My crystal singing bowls and essential oils brought me happiness, and in that happiness, I rediscovered my confidence. I saw more and more clients, hearing spiritual messages through the classical music programs I chose for their journeys. Everything began working together on a spiritual level. I'd begun to enact the positive upward trajectory that was propelling me back to my true purpose.

I was driven to keep that positivity in my life. I got up early every morning to share what I was learning about spirituality and plant healing. I felt I was making a difference in the lives of others again. The oils were an easy way to help more people enhance their connection to their God Presence. I could even predict that the moment they received their oils, something magical would happen in their lives that would bring them into a better place of existence.

As I navigated the path of natural healing and embraced the guidance of God, the dissolution of my marriage became a pivotal and integrated part of this transformative process. Plants played a big part in healing, setting off a chain reaction. The shift in my life happened when I stopped trying to fix the marriage and let God take control.

Dear reader, the secret lies in surrendering to your God presence — the fast track to creating Heaven on Earth.

✳ ✳ ✳

Abundance Sound Bath
and Affirmation Journaling

This practice involves using sound and music to shift your energy towards abundance, followed by a journaling session. Find a quiet, comfortable space where you won't be disturbed, and follow these steps:

1. Set the Atmosphere: Create a serene environment with soft lighting and/or by diffusing essential oils. Choose your sound source, like crystal singing bowls, calming music, or a recorded piece. Try to choose music without words, or with words of another language. (Feel free to visit my website, *www.wellnessmusictherapy.com* or my YouTube channel for music suggestions.) Sit or lie down comfortably, close your eyes, and take several deep breaths to center yourself.

2. Sound Immersion: Start playing the music, allowing the sound vibrations to wash over you. Envision the sound as a radiant, golden light of abundance flowing through your entire being.

3. Abundance Affirmations: While immersed in the sound, silently repeat abundance affirmations:

A. *"I am open to receiving abundance in all areas of my life."*

B. *"Abundance flows to me effortlessly and abundantly."*

C. *"I am a magnet for prosperity and wealth."*

D. *"I attract unlimited abundance into my life now."*

4. Journaling Session: After about 15-20 minutes, turn off the sound source and open your journal. Write down your feelings and experiences during the sound bath. Describe any sensations, thoughts, or visions that arose.

5. Abundance Intentions: Write down specific intentions related to abundance in various areas of your life. These could include financial goals, career aspirations, or personal growth objectives. Be clear and concise about what you want to manifest. Be positive. Write only in positive manifestations.

6. Gratitude Journaling: Express gratitude for the abundance you already have in your life. Write about the blessings, people, or opportunities you're thankful for.

7. Future Abundance Visualization & Surrender: Close your eyes and envision your life brimming with abundance. Picture your goals and intentions materializing. Now, surrender to the light within and let it illuminate your path to manifesting joy, satisfaction, and fulfillment through abundance.

8. Affirmation Reinforcement: Revisit your abundance affirmations and write them down again, reinforcing your commitment to these positive beliefs.

9. Closing and Integration: Conclude your journaling session with a sense of gratitude and optimism. Carry this feeling of abundance with you throughout your day, remaining open to opportunities and abundance.

This practice enhances the power of sound and music with written affirmation reinforcement and visualization. It helps you not only shift your mindset toward abundance but also document your intentions and express gratitude for their existing blessings, fostering a deep sense of abundance in your life.

CHAPTER 5

Embracing Intuition and Healing

*In the symphony of healing, intuition emerges as
the silent conductor, orchestrating the subtle vibrations
of the soul. There is a profound connection between
intuition and the art of healing.*

A TIMELESS saying suggests that every problem has a solution within reach. This can be seen in the relationship between Poison Ivy and Jewelweed, which often grow side by side. Poison Ivy causes a rash, and Jewelweed provides the soothing antidote. This concept applies to our lives as well. The path to healing is closer than we realize, requiring only a curious and creative mind to uncover it.

In my late thirties, as I approached divorce, my solace became the curiosity, joy, and escape I discovered in helping other people. My childhood brush with death had inspired me to continue to be a lifelong student of the Divine.

I became curious about what I didn't know, finding a passion for exploring the medicinal properties of plants and their healing potential. I worked for hours after the kids were asleep. I studied the healing properties of plants, sometimes until four in the morning. As I started to grasp the science of plant healing, I began combining this knowledge with my intuitive gifts.

I started dreaming again, and saw evidence of the Divine in my waking world in the form of lights and colors around people. I started meditating like I'd learned to do in graduate school at Naropa. I facilitated readings with my clients, teaching them how to communicate with their Presence to receive the information they needed. I used music, sound and plants to take them deeper into the process. I discovered an innate knack for choosing essential oils, often discerning client needs even before they expressed them to me. I'd hold my hand over a bottle until I got a telltale tingly feeling. I would choose the oils, then look up the spiritual meaning to share with the client.

This skill deepened my connection with the healing power of Mother Earth. Through intuitive dreams, I gained insights about plants that could benefit my clients. Night after night, I received messages about essential oils needed by clients and promptly gifted them to people. I'd unlocked a new skill: medical intuitiveness.

In one instance, I received a dream message to send citrus fresh, frankincense, and NingXia Red juice to a friend. Two weeks after receiving them, she reached out to express that using the oils had significantly helped with a physical issue she hadn't mentioned previously. This validation was particularly meaningful to me, serving as a humbling affirmation of nature's potential to offer healing gifts, which I had the privilege of sharing.

The process of intuitively identifying plants for emotional, physical and spiritual balance is still mysterious to me. I hover my hand over a group of bottles and patiently wait for that distinct, electrifying energy surging within the palm of my hand, indicating a resonance. Once I choose the oil, I explore the research the spiritual implications and symbolism associated with it. To confirm the accuracy, I then share the spiritual meaning of the oil with the client, consistently finding that it resonates with their personal circumstances. After that, I teach my clients to perform this practice independently, teaching them how to explore the spiritual significance of plants for themselves.

One day my friend Clara asked me to help clear negative energy from her home. I was guided to clear it remotely. I carefully arranged my crystal singing bowls and oils on the floor and called my friend Kris, a seasoned healer, to join me. I held great faith in her knowledge and skills in this realm.

As the clearing began, I followed my intuition and chose an oil, feeling uncertain when I drew Eucalyptus oil. I told my friend who owned the home, that I'd drawn Eucalyptus. I remember saying,

"Of all the 300+ oils that I have, why would that one come up?"

She responded, "Probably because I live on Eucalyptus Street!"

It felt like more than a mere coincidence. We both agreed that this serendipitous oil choice was a validation of the transformative work we were about to do together. Spiritually, the eucalyptus plant has the power to transmute relationships, illuminating connections with oneself, others, work, and the divine. It encourages introspection into the patterns that hinder our progress and sheds light on the dynamics that surface in family interactions or when triggered. She felt as though this message fit for her life at the time. I remember how profound that connection was for all of us. Validation once again.

During the clearing, Kris and I both went into meditation. In my meditation, I heard the faint sound of Debussy's "Clair de Lune" and saw dense energy being drawn up within her home into the realm of light. Then in a moment of clarity, as I played my bowls, a vision unfolded before me — a child from the past, wearing suspenders and a distinctive hat, without arms. I saw the child's mother, patiently awaiting him on the other side, embracing him and guiding him with her into the light. Astonishingly, when Kris and I compared our notes after the clearing, we were both taken aback — we had both seen the *same boy* from a bygone era.

We knew it to be true when we described the boy to each other — a unique image in suspenders with a hat and one major identifier: he had no arms. There still seems to be no plausible way for this vivid detail to manifest independently in both our minds at the same moment.

The composition "Clair de Lune" perfectly captured the

essence of the experience. "Clair de Lune" by Paul Verlaine is a symbolist poem that explores themes of love, beauty, and melancholy in a moonlit night, using dreamy and impressionistic imagery. The composition, through its minor tonality, demonstrates melancholy, while simultaneously conveying a sense of hope to the listener through the imagery and energy of moonlight.

The piece perfectly captured the child/mother reunion that came to me during the clearing. What's even more remarkable is that the clothing in the imagery matched that of the late 19TH century, suggesting a connection to the era in which the child from the vision might have lived.

In the end, Clara shared that the dense energy of the home and strange sounds and interruptions stopped that day. This was a relief for her because those disruptions were the initial reason she reached out to me. It made her feel safer in her home and gave me confidence.

After witnessing numerous spiritual transformations in my sessions, I started sharing the use of oils with other practitioners. Attending annual conferences for music therapists and counselors, I became an expert at demonstrating the use of oils in facilitation, earning recognition from the essential oil company in the form of prizes, jewelry, and even event trips for my achievements.

Yet, despite my excitement and achievements, my husband did not celebrate my successes. In late 2017, I was on the verge of qualifying for an all-expense paid trip for two to

Hawaii due to my success in sharing the power of the oils. Fearful he would discourage me, I had kept this news hidden until the very last moment. On the last night of the contest, I realized I was close to winning the trip to Hawaii and mentioned it to him.

When I told him, he said, "Why would I want to go to Hawaii? I don't want to take off work for that. Who will watch the kids?"

I felt deflated, but he surprisingly agreed to take the kids out to dinner so I could work on it. I doubled down for the next few hours and won the trip. Despite his lack of support, I really wanted to show him what I could do. I thought if he were to come with me, he'd value this part of me. For weeks, he wasn't sure if he would join me on the trip. He reluctantly agreed to join me last minute after the company insisted on his information for travel arrangements, threatening to forfeit his ticket if not provided.

That trip may not have meant much to him, but it marked the beginning of my independence. My business saved me by setting off a chain of events that brought me closer to my path. My business success wasn't solely about achieving financial independence; it also became a wellspring of strength and resilience during the challenging times that awaited me.

I was accumulating light that would return to me in my darkest moments. I had opened a channel for divine guidance to flow through me. How do I know this?

The angels came to me again.

They came to me in the darkest moment, when my husband asked for a financial separation. After this discussion, I found his journal open on the coffee table. It had entries about how to protect his assets during a financial separation. There were notes on how to invest his stocks strategically, a note about deferring his income, a fire sale for the home, and brainstorming what he would do with his extra time. It was eye-opening, to say the least.

He had likely been planning our divorce for years, which explained why he wasn't contributing his whole paycheck to the family. We'd been living on a shoestring budget, with a very small allowance. In the preceding months, I had I discovered a statement for a concealed checking account he had set up in his name. Despite my suspicions, I held trust in him. The most challenging part was dealing with deception. He consistently brushed aside my concerns, labeling them as overreactions whenever I questioned him.

We'd been attending couples therapy, but there was even deceit around the counseling. I distinctly recall a session when the counselor revealed that my husband had met with him privately the week prior. The therapist didn't disclose the details of their private session, but I later discovered they were discussing how he would end the marriage. When I discovered this, I felt so betrayed, as I thought we were in therapy to fix things. As a counselor myself, the non-disclosure from the couples counselor felt like a breach of ethics.

At that point, my husband rarely spoke to me in the

house and often hung up on me when I wanted to talk about anything by phone. He'd disconnected. The story I tell myself is that he had shifted his focus to finding a way to exit our 18-year marriage without facing financial consequences. While it was a devastating realization, it provided the clarity I needed to move forward and start rebuilding my life.

Through it all, I continued to make choices out of *love and not fear*. I chose to view my life through the lens of positivity and hope. I reminded myself that I am loved and have a great purpose. I made the choice to surrender. *Surrendering to reality* is what allowed the angels to come back to me.

The Angels Return

The angels came back to me the evening of that discussion with him. As the reality of the request for financial separation settled in, I found myself in a state of bewilderment, living in an upside-down world. I sat crumpled on the floor, not knowing what to do. A clear message from Source resonated within me: *"Read the books. Meditate."*

Instinctively I knew which books to read — a gift from my new spiritual mentor, Lilia, received two days prior. The moment I received them, I felt a "whoosh" move through me. The books, with their magical aura, radiated comfort and familiarity. As she'd handed them to me, Lilia said:

"These will tell you what the angels are trying to show you."

Holding the century-old books in my hands, I somehow sensed that they would signify the beginning of a mystical journey. In following chapters, I will reveal more about these books. I'll share the wisdom they hold, their role in connecting me with God, and how they serve as a powerful reminder to bring God into every life experience for the betterment of all.

On this night, a few pages in, with tear-filled eyes, I came upon a passage detailing a beautiful light meditation that helped pull me out of devastation after the loss of my marriage. I followed the instructions on the page word for word, first inviting dazzling light to surround my body and entering into stillness in my mind. As I did so, I felt the energy in the room shift. Behind my closed eyes, I knew the room was getting brighter and brighter. I felt an intense connection with my Presence as I read aloud:

"I am a child of the light, I love the light, I live in the light, I serve the light. I am supplied, sustained, illumined and protected by the light. And I bless the light."

As I dedicated my love to the light, I asked for guidance and protection. I begged for clarity and peace. I felt my heart swell like a golden sun.

A flood of insights and realizations washed over me, the first being:

I am of the light and can call upon it at any time.

I sent an outpouring of love into the light, and as I sent adorations and blessings to the light, it surrounded me more, becoming brighter. Amidst heartbreak and despair, I was still protected, illuminated, and supported by the light.

Three giant golden light figures appeared behind me. I

could feel them before I saw them; a weighted, comforting Presence enveloped me, sinking over my skin. I was lifted into the light once again. The three angelic light beings stood behind me, emanating a palpable love that filled me with awe and wonder. They shone brilliantly. It didn't matter who they were — their presence alone was glorious.

One stood tall behind my left shoulder, a shorter one behind my right, and a towering giant in the middle of them. They had one message for me:

"You don't need to be loved by one person to know you are loved."

It was everything I needed to know. And I want you to know it for yourself. Therefore, I share it with you as a great sacred promise that we are all deserving of this love and light.

I cried myself to sleep that night. I lay down next to my sleeping little girl, curled myself into a ball and cried tears of deep gratitude. It's always about coming back to gratitude. I felt blessed to have that connection to the light again, knowing that I was still guided and protected. My experience, no matter how difficult, felt destined to happen.

To the outside world, it might have seemed as if my world was crumbling. Yet, in that moment of darkness, I was honored by a message of unconditional love, realizing without a doubt that it is always available to us. I chose in that moment to trust in the journey and have faith that everything will work out in the end.

Spiritual downloads and messages flooded to me after

that night. The more I read the sacred books and embraced my spirituality, the more light I brought into my life. I leaned on my community to help me through, and gave thanks for everything I experienced, including the hard stuff. I surrounded myself with people who demonstrated compassion, mercy, and understanding. I slowly stopped giving energy to negative people and circumstances that drained me.

I started to share my story in interviews and podcasts, speaking at conferences and posting my healing crystal singing bowl videos on my YouTube channel. I worked with larger groups, leading people through heightened states of consciousness and helping them connect to messages from the Beyond. People told me that my work was giving them hope and reminding them of their brilliance. They felt they had reawakened.

My workshops started filling up. I grew more confident in the messages that I shared, and received constant positive feedback. I had stepped back into my calling.

I'm now deeply entrenched in my spiritual path, building the life I've dreamed of. In sharing my story, Source messages, and teaching people to connect with their Presence, I'm happier than I've ever been. I truly feel alive. I want to help you feel this, too — especially now, when the world needs you most. I want you to feel the freedom of true empowerment and partnership with the Divine.

✻ ✻ ✻

Alchemy of Transformation: Finding Medicine in the Contrast

OBJECTIVE: *To explore challenging situations or aspects of oneself and discover the potential for growth, healing, and transformation within them.*

1. Select a Challenging Situation or Aspect: Begin by choosing a specific situation in your life that you perceive as challenging, or an aspect of yourself that you consider a personal struggle. It could be related to relationships, work, personal habits, or any other area of your life.

2. Reflect on the Poison: Take a few moments to reflect on the negative aspects or difficulties associated with this situation or aspect of yourself. Write down what makes it feel like "poison" in your life. Be honest and open about your feelings and thoughts.

3. Identify Potential Medicine: Now, shift your perspective. Consider the possibility that within this challenging situation or aspect, there might be valuable lessons, growth opportunities, or hidden strengths waiting to be discovered. Write down any insights or potential "medicine" you can find within the "poison."

4. Explore the Lessons: Dive deeper into your reflections. Ask yourself questions like:
- What have I learned from this challenge or aspect of myself?
- How has it contributed to my personal growth or resilience?
- Are there any positive changes or strengths that emerged because of it?

5. Express Gratitude: Regardless of how difficult the situation or aspect may be, express gratitude for the lessons and growth it has brought into your life. Write down your feelings of gratitude and appreciation.

6. Create an Affirmation: Craft a positive affirmation or mantra that encapsulates the transformative aspect of this experience. For example, "I embrace challenges as opportunities for growth and healing."

7. Visualization: Close your eyes and take a few deep breaths. Imagine yourself standing at the edge of a forest, holding a vial labeled "Medicine." In your mind's eye, step into the forest, and as you do, the challenging situation or aspect transforms into a beautiful and vibrant plant, radiating healing energy. Visualize yourself collecting this healing medicine from the plant.

8. Repeat the Affirmation: While still in this visualization, repeat your affirmation several times as you absorb the healing energy from the plant. Feel the positive transformation taking place within you.

9. Journal Your Insights: After the visualization, return to your journal and write down any new insights, feelings of empowerment, or shifts in perspective that have emerged from this practice.

10. Integration: Commit to integrating the newfound perspective and lessons into your life. Whenever you encounter challenges or aspects of yourself that feel like poison, remind yourself of the medicine you've discovered within them.

This practice encourages you to view challenges as opportunities for growth and transformation, emphasizing the potential for positive change even in the most difficult situations. Over time, it can help you develop a more resilient and empowered mindset. As you go to sleep nightly, think of all you are grateful for.

CHAPTER 6

Awakening to Divine Signs

*What if the key to life is learning to connect with the
divine source, creating in harmony with the universe?
What if every thought, every action weaves threads
of co-creation, shaping our reality?*

IN THE year leading up to the divorce, I had blocked the messages coming through. Source responded to my resistance by bringing me bigger challenges, forcing me to rebuild my life from the ground up. Sometimes it must happen this way, but I believe that recognizing signs earlier could have prevented the rug being pulled out from under me. It's only in hindsight that I realize that I could have listened *sooner*. Therefore, I've since learned the practice of attentively listening and actively searching for the messages of God in every experience — an essential lesson I aim to impart in this chapter.

The warning messages began early on January 3, 2018, while I was filling the tub to take a bath. As the tub was filling, my son yelled from downstairs: "Mom! Come quick! There's water coming through the ceiling!"

I ran downstairs to see water streaming out of the bottom of a light fixture onto the wood floors in the kitchen. I grabbed a pot to catch the water and ran up to turn off the faucet. I drained the tub and looked at it, completely baffled. The tub looked to be intact. I had no idea of the source of the mysterious leak.

A few weeks later, a plumber found a hairline horizontal crack in the tub that caused water to leak into the ceiling when the tub was filled. The crack would open under pressure, allowing water to enter the framework. As the water spilled over and the pressure decreased, the crack closed up again, appearing undamaged.

After the initial tub leak and water damage was repaired, more leaks appeared in different parts of the house and this continued for months. When a roof leak was discovered while removing the baseboards, I began to hear the message,

"You can fix the leaks, but you can't fix the marriage."

Then, a new roof leak occurred a few weeks later, causing water to pour into the entryway. Again came the message.

Then, as the construction crew was draining the water, the drain hose fell out of the kitchen sink and flooded another part of the house, leading to more repairs. Just when I thought everything was almost fixed, they turned on the water and two of the toilets had a gasket failure, causing more damage. The message was now daily and insistent:

"You can fix the leaks, but you can't fix the marriage."

I didn't pay much attention to the message, and Source

responded by creating more situations to emphasize the message. Unaware, I would casually dismiss it with a breath, shake my head, and wonder where the thought came from.

I convinced myself that nothing was wrong. I even found myself growing frustrated, believing the recurring messages were a manifestation of my own insecurities and fear-driven thinking. In the end, it didn't help to ignore the voice of God. It all was going to happen as it was meant to happen.

Those months were exhausting. There were 248 days of repairs and renovations, peppered with that all-too-familiar booming from construction every few days. The messages continued to resurface intermittently, serving as a simple reminder. I became excellent at ignoring it. That is, until things started escalating.

Somewhere in the middle of constant repairs, new floors, baseboard paint and bathroom fixtures, I found respite in attending a networking meeting where I was delighted to see one of my spiritual friends, Siobhan.

She had shared a vision with me a few months prior — a vision that was accurate. At the time, we were chatting while watching our kids play together, and I discussed my business goals. Back then, I was striving to achieve the coveted gold rank within my company. It was an exciting period, as I was not only pursuing that goal but also preparing for an upcoming workshop. The workshop aimed to explore the potential of oils, crystal singing bowls, and affirmations in manifesting abundance.

I had not shared any details about the workshop with

Siobhan, yet she picked up on it. She got all excited and said that there was a golden being with us "peeking through the veil."

I was delighted to hear this, as I'd not even asked at all for any type of reading. She said, "I see him holding a bottle of oil with gold flecks in it." She was spot on. I achieved the rank of Gold a couple of weeks later.

This is why, as soon as she walked up to me at the networking event, my face lit up and I gave her a big hug. Without blinking, she asked: "Do you know what water means?"

I was taken aback. I'd not shared with her about the water leaks and at my home, but then again, I was not surprised that she knew about it. I told her that I thought I knew because I had actually looked into it. I'd hired a Feng Shui expert, thinking perhaps we needed to clear the energy in the home.

I asked her if what I'd learned was correct: that water was a reflection of negative energy in my home that needed to be cleared.

She said "It's not that at all. Water represents withheld emotion."

I was not expecting to hear that answer, but perhaps it was the answer I was looking for. I internalized it, thinking I needed to be more clear about *my feelings*. I dove into more inner work, hoping to turn the leaks around. I started listening to the messages and taking action to understand what Source was trying to tell me. I was ready to do whatever it took.

I took it a step further. I created a daily practice to seek more information from Source. I established a ritual that involved the use of Young Living essential oils, each paired with corresponding spiritual questions derived from my study of *A Course in Miracles* (ACIM - Foundation for Inner Peace).

The oils were called *Freedom, Valor, Divine Release, Inner Harmony, TR Care, Transformation, Joy,* and *Aromasleep.* Following the Young Living protocol, I used *Valor* on my feet for courage, *Joy* on my heart for love, *Divine Release* on my head for spiritual support, and *Inner Harmony* over my throat and wrists to support my voice.

I then changed the oils I was using after the first 30 days. Per the protocol on the Freedom Collection, I then used *Freedom* on my feet, *Transformation* on my throat and *TR Care* on my ears for added support. For two months, twice a day, I placed the oils on my body, asking these questions with every application:

"Where would You have me go?"

"What would You have me do?"

"What would You have me say, and to whom?"

—Workbook Lesson 71, A COURSE IN MIRACLES

I first noticed I was sleeping significantly better. I felt more rested, and my sleep app said I was getting more REM sleep. I felt more calm and protected during the day. It was during this practice, before the divorce, when I started noticing more of the dysfunction in my relationship. As if looking through a camera, I observed reality in a focused way. The oils kept me balanced, so I could have an objective view.

The signs were everywhere, and I was finally beginning to

listen. It was like a symphony of events leading to the grand finale. Everything was set in motion for the forest to burn, and for me to have the tools necessary to rise from the ashes. Had I read the signs earlier, maybe things would have been different. However, I like to believe it happened just as it was meant to happen so I could teach others how to read the signs, as well.

After the angels came back to me, I again became a student of my spiritual experience. My world was crumbling so it could be rebuilt in the most beautiful way. The signs circled around me, guiding me towards a brighter future. These signs had always been there, but I needed to rise above my human struggle to hear them. It required a shift in perspective, learning to acknowledge their origin from a higher power.

It was as if floodgates opened to let my authentic self emerge. The freedom to be unapologetically me elevated my spiritual work, establishing a new connection with my Presence. At times, the words flowing from my mouth in workshops were guided by a higher source. I was flooded with *so many* messages that I literally couldn't keep them to myself.

Guiding Clients: Sharing Divine Messages

My client Jules resonated so profoundly with my newfound spiritual messages that she traveled an hour and a half every week to journey through music with me. One day, as I was prepping for one of her sessions, the image of an elderly woman dressed in a white top came to me. She held three white roses in front of her. I could only see her from the chest up, and noticed a man standing behind her left shoulder. He was wearing a pastel yellow button-down shirt, had light red-brown hair and a mustache. I felt a sense of confusion that turned to humor as they appeared before me, and the phrase "gluten-free meatloaf" came to me. I dismissed it for the moment and continued to prepare for the session.

I remember knowing it was a message for her, but I didn't know if I was brave enough to share it. I wanted to maintain professionalism. I sat through the session and stayed present with her as the image of the woman and man came back to me over and over as I worked up the courage to share the message at the end of the session. After all, she was paying money for a healing session, not a reading.

As we were wrapping up, I said: "I have something strange to ask you. This morning, as I was getting ready, a vision came to me of a woman and a man. The woman was older, with white hair and a soft face. She was holding three white roses and smiling. The man was in a yellow button-down shirt. He had reddish-brown hair, and a mustache. Does this mean anything to you?"

She gasped and smiled. "Ellen! Yes!" she replied. "My mother and brother! This is wonderful! I *need* to tell you what happened with three white roses yesterday! I was walking along the boardwalk and one of the shops was having a going out of business sale. They were giving away white roses as a sign of appreciation for the patrons that had supported them over the years. When it came time to choose my rose, I asked if I could have three. The woman said they were almost closed, so I could feel free to take them. I chose three white roses to represent myself, my brother and my mother, who have both passed on. I took the three roses to the church next door and placed them on the altar."

We realized at that moment that her mother and brother had come through as a sign of validation. They had received her offering and wanted her to know that they were still with her. I explained that they were happy and complete on the other side.

Then I asked whether "gluten free meatloaf" meant anything to her.

She said: "Actually, yes! We used to joke that my mother made the *original* gluten free meatloaf because she didn't put breadcrumbs in her recipe."

At that moment, I realized that these spiritual messages were a gift meant to be shared for the greater good, for healing, and for hope. It is not my mission to filter or hold back messages. I started sharing more and more, gaining the confidence I needed that eventually contributed to my own healing.

As this major shift was happening for me, similar shifts unfolded for people around the world, as we learned amidst global lockdown to embrace a deeper spiritual version of ourselves. This period may have brought about the end of relationships, health or careers but also saw the emergence of a beautiful and vulnerable rediscovery of the self.

Take a moment to think back on your own life and reflect

on the changes you have experienced in the last three to four years. My guess is that you never would have predicted where you are now. With the perspective of time, think about how life changes unfolded in your relationships, and see the positive shifts that came from those shifts. Did releasing negative influences give way to higher frequency connections, uplifting friendships, or partnerships? Similarly, if you encountered the end of a career, look back and consider the good that came of it — an opportunity for self-reflection and redirection.

These moments in your past invited you to recreate yourself, rising to a new level of existence. If this is happening in your life, know that you are on the right path. It tends to unfold for each of us when we are ready to make the conscious choice to align with higher frequencies of being. Wherever you are in this journey, take comfort. In every case that I've known, when the dust settles, this shift provides for a more positive life experience.

Now, let's address how to tap into signs of impending change to make shifts in your life without having to go through the kind of hard lessons I experienced. By using free will to act on the messages we receive, we demonstrate to Source that we are actively listening and integrating the messages. This intentional engagement enhances the connection, allowing Source to give us more of what we desire. I've heard some refer to it as the Law of Balance.

The first step is to invite your higher Presence to support you in this process. Remember, Presence is always waiting for you to reach out and ask for help. Once you've made the call and released control to your God Presence, you will be amazed at how information starts to flow to you.

Why does it work? Because you are taking action by shifting your thoughts and intentions, while also asking Source to assist you. This is a powerful demonstration of your readiness to co-create with Divine Love.

How can you tell if you are receiving Divine messages? There will be signs that validate your progress, and it's important to be aware of them as you continue to practice. Here are some of the signs that you may experience:

- A sudden "knowing" or intuition
- Physical sensations such as chills, tingling, or rushes of energy
- Seeing sparkles, colors, or flashes of light
- Heightened sensitivity to temperature or sound
- Feeling disconnected or dispassionate
- Changes in taste or cravings for food
- Digestion changes or sudden weight fluctuations
- Increased awareness of emotions, such as loneliness or isolation
- Shifts in energy levels, including feeling the need for more rest or being wide awake despite lack of sleep
- Newfound intolerance to negative or low-vibrational people or things
- Feeling drawn to nature or more natural environments

- Significant changes in life circumstances, such as a new career or move to a different location.

Remember that these signs are unique to each individual, and there may be other indicators that you're on the right path. Trust in the process and have faith that the universe is guiding you towards your highest good.

Meditation opened the door to a world of intuitive shifts and insights for me. During one session, a clear message came through: stop eating red meat. I followed this guidance and soon noticed a shift in my connection to nature. Being outside filled me with energy, and I could feel nature's presence in my body, like the sensation of music. My relationship with the natural world transformed entirely, and I felt as though I was entering into a partnership with Mother Earth.

Some other common signs of spiritual expansion include chance encounters with unusual or meaningful people, as well as experiencing more synchronicities in life. Many people notice shifts in their sleep patterns or dreams. They find themselves with increased energy at night and waking up frequently between 2-4 a.m. As psychic abilities develop, intuition may become heightened and interference in electrical appliances may occur. Devices may malfunction when you are in a heightened state of emotion or are nearby. For me, light bulbs may flicker or blow out when I am near, and streetlamps often turn off or on as I walk or drive by.

Emotionally, you may experience feelings of love, recognizing moments of deep gratitude, appreciation, peace, clarity, understanding, and compassion. You may find that your in-sights for friends and family are more on point when you share them, and start to recognize the oneness in everything, finding unexpected synchronicities in the world. Many will notice the repetition of certain numbers on a clock, like 11:11 or 2:22, and somehow feel drawn to look at the clock during these times. Others sense encounters with angelic and cosmic beings, increasing their awareness of the presence of loving energies.

Some feel like they don't fit on earth anymore, a feeling often eased by spending time in nature. It's not Earth itself that feels distant, but the human-made systems imposed on it. Another sign is that you discover a quiet part of you that wants to reconnect with ancient wisdom. Any of these feel-ings or "symptoms" of spiritual awakening are signs that you are ready to start a new human experience, one that is more aligned with God. Other signs of spiritual expansion include seeing geometric symbols.

As you become more aware of these signs and symbols, your spiritual experiences will deepen. By choosing positiv-ity and shedding negativity, you become a beacon of light for others seeking guidance. We are fortunate to be alive during this new Golden Age and have the opportunity to help oth-ers realize their potential. By releasing limiting beliefs, we can manifest our dreams for the greater good. Later in the book, I will discuss how the mind is a powerful tool for attaining higher consciousness.

Many of us have found that a spiritual awakening or "initiation" is not an easy time. We find that distractions are removed from our lives and we are forced to look at ourselves. We may even lose the ability to exercise, or lose friends or family relationships that have brought stability to us in the past. We may find that old habits of distraction no longer work. Everything from our work to our health may be affected, depending on our path and how it was predetermined. Many ask, "What do I do when the rug has been pulled out from under me?"

This is where the power of choice and the Law of Balance come in. According to my understanding of the Law of Balance, as we progressively align with our individual paths and rely more on our higher Presence, we strengthen our connections and communication with Source. Taking action is the way we demonstrate to the Divine that we are receptive and engaged. This action based on spiritual connection leads us to a life filled with joy, which contributes to the well-being of not only our personal world but also our communities.

As you start to learn to manifest, you must remember that support cannot come through without the conscious call for it. When you ask for help, you show that you are listening and working in partnership with Source. There are many ways to do this.

I always start with gratitude. I ask myself:

"What is the gift in this situation?"

When I start to see the gifts, my perspective shifts entirely.

I can then see the purpose behind my hardships. In working with author Jack Canfield, I have learned so much about my path, and have defined the questions that I need to ask of myself. Jack is the beloved author of the *Chicken Soup for the Soul* series, and one of America's favorite coaches and mentors. I began working with him as a mentor after sharing my crystal singing bowl practice with his team. I've learned so much through his mentorship about the practice of abundance, manifestation, and perspective. I've learned to ask myself:

- *"What if I chose this situation before I came here?"*
- *"What if I had a contract to have this circumstance happen exactly as it is happening right now?"*
- *"What if this was all supposed to happen this way?"*

Do you see how these questions can change our perspective? Simply ask, "How can I learn *through this* to help others who might go through the same thing?" It instantly releases victim mentality. By asking these questions, we often start to shift instantly.

※ ※ ※

Discovering Your Intuition and Following Signs

Step 1: Setting Your Intention and Affirmations. Begin by finding a quiet and comfortable space where you can focus your thoughts and energy. Take a few deep breaths to center yourself.

Step 2: Meditation and Deep Connection. Once you have your intention in mind, move into a state of meditation. Use your knowledge of deep meditation techniques to quiet your mind and open yourself to higher frequencies.

Imagine yourself surrounded by pure, radiant light. Feel this light permeate every cell of your being, raising your vibrational frequency. Visualize your intention as a glowing beacon within this light, shining brightly in the universe.

Step 3: Vocal Toning for Higher Frequency. As you bask in this elevated state of consciousness, let your voice resonate with the intentions you've set. Allow the tones to ripple through your body, aligning you with the frequencies of your desires. Try different vowel sounds until you find one that resonates the body and creates a calm, relaxing feeling within.

Step 4: Request a Clear Sign from the Universe. Now, with your intention and affirmations firmly in mind, take a moment to ask the universe for a clear and specific sign that will confirm you are on the right path. This step is crucial because it sets the stage for the universe to provide you with unmistakable guidance.

To harness the full power of this practice, it's important to be as specific as possible about the sign you want to receive. Your choice of a sign should resonate deeply with you, carrying personal meaning or significance. Here are some examples of specific signs you might request:

1. ANIMAL TOTEM: You could choose a particular animal that holds symbolism or meaning in your life. For instance, if you have a strong connection with eagles, you might request to see an eagle as your sign.

2. SONG ON THE RADIO: If music is a profound part of your life, you could ask for a specific song to play on the radio at an unexpected moment. This song should have lyrics or a message that aligns with your intention.

3. NUMBER SEQUENCE: Many people find meaning in number sequences, such as 111, 333, or 777. You might ask to see

a specific number sequence at a significant time or place.

4. NATURE ELEMENT: Choose a natural element like a rainbow, a shooting star, or a specific flower that resonates with you. Request to encounter this element when you most need confirmation.

5. COINCIDENTAL ENCOUNTER: It could be a particular person, a book, or a place that holds significance in your life. Ask to come across this element unexpectedly and in a way that leaves no doubt it's a sign.

6. SPECIFIC PHRASE OR WORD: Choose a word or phrase that carries deep meaning for you. Request to see or hear this phrase in a context that reaffirms your intention.

Why Specificity Matters: Being specific about the sign you request serves two essential purposes. First, it deepens your connection to the sign because it holds personal significance. Second, it makes it easier for you to recognize the sign when it appears, reducing the likelihood of misinterpretation.

Trust the Universe: Once you've made your specific request, trust that the universe is listening and working to align the circumstances to deliver your sign. Avoid trying to control or force the sign's appearance; instead, maintain a sense of openness and receptivity.

Keeping a Journal: As you go through this practice, consider keeping a journal dedicated to your manifestations and signs. Note down the specific sign you've requested, your experiences during meditation and vocal toning, and any signs or synchronicities you encounter in your daily life. Journaling helps you track your progress, recognize patterns, and build confidence in the manifestation process.

Step 5: Gratitude and Releasing Expectations. After making your request, express gratitude to the universe for its guidance and support. Gratitude amplifies the power of your intentions. Release any expectations about when or how the sign will appear. Trust that the universe's timing is perfect, and the sign will manifest when it's most aligned with your journey.

Step 6: Daily Affirmations and Integration. In the days that follow, continue to affirm your intention daily, reinforcing your connection with the desired manifestation.

Step 7: Recognizing the Sign. Keep a keen eye on your surroundings, experiences, and interactions. Be open to receiving the sign you requested, and when it appears, trust your intuition and inner guidance to recognize it. The sign may come in unexpected ways, so stay attuned to synchronicities and subtle messages from the universe.

Step 8: Reflect and Take Inspired Action. Upon receiving your sign, take time to reflect on its meaning and how it aligns with your intention. Let it guide your actions and decisions. As a spiritual coach, you understand the importance of inspired action, so allow the sign to lead you toward the manifestation of your desires.

CHAPTER 7

A Phone Call from God

*Even the subtlest signs may resonate as spiritual notations
from the universe — a cosmic whisper, inviting us to
reawaken to the wisdom of our souls.*

ABOUT TWO months before my husband asked for a financial separation, I was enjoying a summer day in July, getting ready to take my children to a concert at Moonlight Beach in Encinitas, California. Little did I know that day would mark a turning point in my life. As I was packing snacks and gathering towels, I received a phone call from a number I didn't recognize. Something told me to answer amidst the preparations.

Lilia Samoilo, a woman I'd never met but knew instantly, introduced herself and told me that she had come across my near-death experience on YouTube three years prior, and that the Ascended Masters had told her to call me that very day. While others might be skeptical, something in her voice captivated me. I felt that I already knew her somehow. As she spoke about her connection to Source, I found myself fascinated by her messages of love and expansion. She knew many others who had near death experiences and told me I might like to connect with IANDS, the International Association for Near Death Studies. After we hung up, I felt a sense of gratitude and a strong desire to learn more about her and her work.

I spoke to Lilia several times over the next couple of days. She was curious about my experiences and asked me questions about the messages I received while in Heaven. We dove into discussions about the Ascended Masters, including my encounters with Jesus and Buddha, and Lilia shared her own experiences.

Lilia, an experienced spiritual teacher with over forty years dedicated to studying sacred spiritual teachings, had been studying and practicing the Cosmic Laws of the universe, the "I AM" Instruction for over forty years found in the Saint Germain Series Books. (She was promised these books during her NDE at age three and found them at age nineteen.) Since her first near-death experience as a toddler, she had received messages and worked directly with the Ascended Masters. In essence, she had been studying the I AM Discourses, the ancient spiritual works that came to me, for as long as I had been alive. Her purpose on Earth was clear — to teach people about living in their light by learning the power of connecting with their God Presence.

In her own words, Lilia shared why she reached out to me. "My heart recognized you in a video I saw of you sharing your NDE, and I saved it for years. One day, in the summer of 2019, I came across that video, felt an unexplainable connection, and was told to "find you."

What she did not know was that I had asked God for an answer, and astonishingly she called me *just twelve hours later*. During our conversation, she encouraged me to share my Near-Death Experience (NDE) with the public. She shared later that she sensed a serious issue concerning my marriage, adding to the significant reasons she was guided to contact me. The timing was perfect, and Lilia stepped in precisely when needed.

Months later, as I began receiving more spiritual messages, I heard the following:

"Lilia is one of us. She was placed here to remind you of the Cosmic Law. She works with many, always with great love for her children. She knew as a baby what she was here to do and has never faltered. Her job is difficult, as humans have limited sight. There is only so much humans can understand at a time, which takes them away from their calling. She loves the validation from you and other students because it gives her strength and perseverance to carry on. Lilia is special. She taught us."

Lilia's connection to the Divine was undeniable. Her ability to sense when I needed her support, even though we lived miles apart, was truly remarkable. There were times when I received messages in a dream and Lilia would synchronistically call me out of the blue, even when my memory of the experience was hazy. It was as if she had a direct line to the

Universe. I feel blessed to have her in my life.

Soon after my first conversation with Lilia, she invited me to join her at an IANDS conference on the East Coast. The conference was a little over two weeks away, and I didn't see any possible way that I would be able to attend. After all, I was a mother of three, and my husband wasn't particularly supportive of me working or traveling. She said, "Let's leave it to the Masters and release it to your Presence to find a way."

Surprisingly, my husband supported my decision to attend the conference. In a wonderful twist, I discovered that Lilia had prayed about it and received a message that the path would be cleared. To make it financially feasible, I decided to host a booth to share the spiritual uses of Young Living Essential Oils.

When I arrived at the IANDS conference, my cousin Heidi was waiting for me at the hotel. We were co-hosting the booth, and she had arrived to help me set up. Despite not knowing much about my spiritual gifts, Heidi is quite intuitive and was about to receive a crash course in spirituality. Once everything was set up, we headed back to the hotel to unwind.

When I checked into our room, I sensed a powerful, positive energy vibrating throughout my body. The vibration was so intense that I was visibly shaking. To allow the energy to flow freely and invite all that was for the greater good, I consciously created a blue bubble of light and requested space to rest until I was ready to tap in more fully in the morning. I should have known then that something amazing was about to happen.

The next morning when I stepped into the hall, I felt at home. The energy was warm and weighted, similar to the light on the other side. The hall had no windows, but it felt light and was surrounded by other Near-Death Experiencers. I knew on a cellular level that they understood my journey. I relaxed because I could just be myself. I let down my walls and all at once received the message:

"You are a student."

At the time, I believed that meant I was a student of the conference. However, a gift from Lilia would soon clarify that the message meant something much bigger for my life journey. Not yet knowing the full extent of the message, I embraced my role as a student of the conference, and started to observe the world around me with a newfound awareness.

As I stood at our oils booth, I listened intently to everyone who stopped by, asking them about their near-death experience. I felt instantly connected to them. Dozens of other Experiencers came to visit, and I focused on their energy, seeing energy move in ways I had never seen before. In addition, in the conference hall, I was surrounded by books about angels and those who had also touched Heaven. It was so magical to be in the midst of it all. I put oils on people, flowed loving energy through them by holding my hands with oils over their heads, called in the light, and let God take the lead.

As I shared my near-death experience with others, I was fascinated to learn that my story had similarities to NDEs

reported in other cultures. One researcher explained that
many Japanese NDEs involve starting on a vessel or boat of
some type, which closely resembles how I found myself on a
wooden raft. In connecting with other experiencers, I felt a
deep sense of affirmation and connection with those who had
gone through similar encounters.

It was in this conference hall that I first saw "The Veil,"
and I remember turning to Heidi and asking if she saw the
same white light in the room. Soon after seeing the veil, Lilia
walked into the room.

That day, Lilia came forward with an answer to *my call*.
It was a call to God that I'd almost forgotten about entirely.
Just before she'd called me that beautiful summer day, I'd asked
the Universe to help me understand more about the angels.
At the time, light beings had been coming to me in my workshops in different formations. I'd see them around the circle,
either next to participants or in different arrangements, such
as concentric circles or standing stoically in straight rows.
Sometimes they brought animals into the center of the circle.
Sometimes I saw light beings and Ascended Masters. It was
during one of these circles that I asked God to teach me what
the angels were trying to show me.

When Lilia walked up to me with three books in hand
and a huge smile on her face, I felt a deep remembrance. The
books in her hands were very old, and green with gold em-
bossing. When I touched them, I felt a rush of emotional and
spiritual energy. I was instantly overwhelmed with gratitude

and started crying; it felt as if they were returning to me. With an answer to my prayer, she handed them to me and said:

"These will tell you what the angels have been trying to show you."

Exploring Divine Guidance and Spiritual Connections

EXERCISE 1: Divine Messages

Reflect on moments in your life when you received what you believe to be divine guidance or messages. Choose one significant experience.

- Describe the circumstances and feelings associated with this experience.
- Reflect on how it influenced your life path.

EXERCISE 2: Unanswered Calls

Recall a time when you felt a strong inner calling but didn't follow through. Choose one such moment.

- Describe the situation and why you didn't act on the calling.
- Reflect on whether you still feel a connection to that calling and whether there are any actions you can take now.

EXERCISE 3: Connecting with Spiritual Teachers

Think about encounters with spiritual teachers or guides in your life, or imagine such a meeting.

- Describe a memorable encounter or visualize one.
- Reflect on the wisdom or lessons you gained from these encounters.

Integration and Insights: Consider how these experiences have shaped your spiritual journey.

- Identify common themes or lessons from these encounters.
- Reflect on any unresolved aspects of your spiritual path.
- Explore how you can actively seek divine guidance in your current life.

This condensed exercise allows you to explore divine guidance, unanswered calls, and spiritual connections in a more concise manner, providing insights into their impact on your spiritual journey.

CHAPTER 8

How a Psychic's Revelation Predicted My Path

Intuitive gifts, when embraced, can become guiding instruments for good. They illuminate the path to a connection with our inner selves, empowering us to enter into conversations with God.

THE CONFERENCE was a gathering of healers, psychics, and authors, all sharing their NDEs and experiences with light beings and Ascended Masters. I was delighted to share the oils and during breaks, I reveled in the chance to talk with other exhibitors. Among them was Jane, a psychic with extraordinary gifts, and her husband, a skeptic-turned-believer who was the epitome of love and support. I watched as he set up her table and took appointments. He brought her food and spoke of her with deep love. I was transfixed since it had been awhile since I had seen this type of loving adoration between partners. They showed me how Divine partnership could work and foreshadowed a glimpse of my future.

On the second to last day, before the gift of books from

Lilia, I received an intuitive reading from Jane. Having never experienced a paid reading before, I decided to invest in a 15-minute session during a quiet moment at the conference. At the time, I had no desire to leave my marriage. I had resigned to working on it for the rest of my life.

The timing of the universe was impeccable, as my life was going to change within a mere 24 hours of her reading.

Jane started with: *"Ok, honey, your husband will never fully understand what you came here to do. Go home and write a letter to him, focusing on the positive parts of your relationship. Write the things you loved about him when you met. Write what attracted you... all positive."*

Two days after receiving those instructions and the day after returning home from the conference, I wrote that letter to him. It was the beginning of my return to myself. I had put off writing it all day, and it wasn't until early evening that I finally convinced myself to do it. I wrote everything she suggested, completely unaware of what was about to happen. I wrote about the qualities that had initially attracted me to him and expressed gratitude for our children and life together. Then I went to sign my name.

The moment I signed my name to the letter was exactly when my husband walked through the front door and said, "We need to talk."

I grabbed the letter and followed him upstairs. I sat across from him, the air feeling thick between us.

The conversation hit me like a truck. This was when he

requested a financial separation, wanting to live apart, share custody of the children and keep our finances separate. He had no desire to continue to work on the relationship.

My heart was heavy in my chest; I could barely comprehend what was happening. My first thought was: *What about the kids?* I reeled with emotions, frozen to the chair I was sitting in. I had so many questions. It felt like my human mind had to catch up with the scenario my Soul had anticipated. The time had arrived.

I looked down at the letter, still feeling numb, not knowing what to do next. I handed it to him, somehow knowing I wouldn't have the strength to give it to him later.

He took the letter and went downstairs to take a shower, leaving his journal on the table. It was then that I looked down and saw notes about "deferred income" and a "fire" sale of the house. More shock set in as I realized the strategy around the choice he'd made. This was about money.

When he came out of the shower, armed with this new information, I asked him: "If you don't want to work on it, then why do you want a financial separation, instead of a divorce?"

His reply: "In case I change my mind."

It hit me again. What had I been doing? I had consciously remained in a loveless marriage, disregarding my own needs for love. When I heard his answer, I thought: *"Why am I waiting for him to choose? I have a choice, too."*

Despite having convinced myself that I would never leave, I couldn't willingly remain where love had faded. Our

time together had run its course. It was time to leave and begin a new chapter, where I could finally be my true self. This
was the night when the angels visited me, an experience I've
detailed earlier in this book.

I filed for divorce a day later. Jane, the psychic, called me
that very morning. She called to invite me to participate in
an upcoming psychology conference, and I told her that there
was no way I could consider it because of the impending divorce. She surprised me by saying:

*"Ok, honey, I saw this coming. You could never do the work
you are meant to do in this lifetime with him by your side. Here's
my advice to you. Always look forward, never look back and hire
an attorney to protect yourself. This is your reawakening."*

She went on:

*"There's a great love on the other side of this. He's been waiting
for you. You will have a beautiful life with him. It will be a more
beautiful than you can ever possibly imagine."*

During my initial reading at the conference, Jane hadn't
told me what she foresaw for my future, and I'm glad she
didn't. It was important for me to live through those experiences as part of my journey.

Adjusting to my new reality, her words brought comfort,
and I began sharing my spiritual gifts with the world. She boosted my confidence by seeking messages from me, and as we ex-
changed insights about the world, I felt honored by her trust.
Stepping beyond the ordinary, I embraced my connection with
the light realms. Sharing visions and dreams became a part of

my calling.

One early example stands out in my memory. While getting my nails done, a vision of a young six-year-old girl in pink, holding a frilly parasol, entered my consciousness. Despite attempting to dismiss it, she persisted in coming to me. Taking a leap of faith, I asked the woman tending to my hands if she was open to receiving spiritual messages.

"I see a six-year-old girl in pink, holding a pink parasol. Does this mean anything to you?"

I braced myself for any reaction, fearing I might have overstepped. To my surprise, she gazed at me intensely and asked:

"Can you see her *now?*"

Relieved, I told her yes.

What she told me next was both poignant and heartwrenching — her daughter had passed away at the age of six, and it would have been her 21st birthday the previous weekend. She shared that she had visited her daughter's grave with gifts of remembrance just days before.

With her confirmation, a flood of messages poured into my consciousness.

"Your family has been concerned. There is no need to fear. Everything will work out. You are well protected."

Her eyes welled up with tears as I continued,

"She does not come to you, but she comes to another in your family through dreams. Her sister."

It was then that she revealed her late daughter was a twin,

and her twin sister still lived. A wave of chills swept over me as I conveyed more messages of hope and reassurance that came through. I reminded her to connect with her Presence. The encounter was a gift, allowing me to offer comfort during a difficult time. I reassured her once again that she was surrounded by light and love, reminding her that everything would work out.

With a heart full of gratitude, I paid and left, thankful for the ability to share such a beautiful moment. After all, I don't always see loved ones who have passed. Yet, in that sacred moment, I knew that the purpose of that experience was not about what I saw; rather, it was a calling to help this woman find peace in connecting with her own higher Presence. Whatever comes is a gift to help others rediscover their own wisdom, and rekindle their faith in the Divine.

Writing Your Letter of Reflection

This exercise is designed to help you engage in a profound act of self-reflection and gratitude. You will write a heartfelt letter to yourself or someone else, focusing on the positive aspects of a relationship, even if it has evolved or ended. This exercise can bring closure, healing, and a renewed perspective on the connections in your life.

1. Select the Recipient: Decide whether you want to write this letter to yourself or to someone else who has played a significant role in your life. It could be a current or past partner, friend, family member, or mentor. Choose the option that resonates most with you.

2. Set the Tone: Begin the letter with a warm and sincere greeting. If you're writing to yourself, address it as if you are writing to your past self or your future self. If writing to someone else, address them by name.

3. Express Gratitude: Share your gratitude for the positive qualities, experiences, or lessons associated with the person or relationship. Be specific about what you appreciate. Consider the following prompts:
- What unique qualities or strengths did this person possess?
- How did this relationship contribute to your personal growth or happiness?
- What memorable moments or experiences did you share?

4. Reflect on Growth: Use this opportunity to reflect on how this person or relationship has influenced your life journey. Consider how you've evolved, what you've learned, and the impact it has had on your character.
- Describe the ways in which your life has been transformed through this connection.
- Share any insights or realizations you've gained as a result of this relationship.
- Reflect on the positive changes or personal growth that occurred during or after your time together.

5. Closing with Grace: Conclude the letter with a message of appreciation and closure. Even if the relationship has evolved or ended, express your best wishes and gratitude for the part they've played in your life.
- Offer a heartfelt closing statement that leaves room for future growth and understanding.

- If writing to yourself, consider giving advice or encouragement for your future self.

6. Seal the Letter: After completing your letter, take a moment to reread it and ensure it conveys your feelings accurately. Then, sign and date it.

7. Share or Keep Private: Decide whether you want to share the letter with the intended recipient or keep it as a personal reflection. The choice is yours, and both options can be meaningful.

Writing this letter can be a therapeutic and illuminating experience. It allows you to acknowledge the positive aspects of relationships, find closure if needed, and embrace the transformative power of gratitude and reflection in your life.

CHAPTER 9

From Past Lives to Cosmic Visions

When you look for magic, you start to see it everywhere.

MANY have asked if I believe in past lives. I can't say that I did before my head injury, but I came back with a "knowing" after I woke up. The message? "This ain't my first rodeo!" This awareness was validated over the course of mystical experiences since then.

One of the most eye-opening past life experiences I had was during a weekend training on holotropic breathwork, a process of intense active breathing that can be used as a tool to deal with past trauma. In the training we were paired with a partner, and I witnessed my colleague travel back in time to a traumatic event in her life. She relived the moment through the breathwork, as the trainers guided and supported her. It was like watching magic at work.

When my turn came, I remained open to the process, but secretly hoped the breathwork would help me access the memories that I'd lost due to my head injury. At that point in my life,

I was almost desperate to remember my childhood. I was told by the trainers to let that expectation go and allow my body, the breath, and Source to lead me to what I needed to know.

As I closed my eyes and began to move into the breath, dramatic sensations washed over me. Vivid images of past lives flooded my mind, each offering a glimpse of myself experiencing death in different embodiments. However, in place of fear or panic, I held a sense of detachment. I dispassionately observed that I died from a head injury over and over, in countless lifetimes.

In one lifetime, I died from a head injury when I fell from a horse, sometime in early American history. In another, I was a Native American, killed by a bullet from an American soldier's gun. The visions came and went, granting a new understanding: my present life held the opportunity to end this cycle. I was given the opportunity to let go of old karmic ties and overcome the patterns that had been holding me back for a long time. As I reflected on the gift of living this life, and the synchronicities between my head injury and how I'd passed in other lives, I found myself embracing this life more fully.

The following experience, which occurred during a friend's housewarming ceremony, acted as another powerful validation for me. It revealed to me that we are on more than an earthly journey and our purpose is more than just learning for our soul expansion. It's about interconnectedness. We have parts of the puzzle to share with each other. The ceremony was led by her spiritual guru, and during the meditation, I had a vision. I saw a baby elephant still inside its water sac, as if it were just being born. This image then transformed into another, and I found myself holding a large staff with a beautiful blue gemstone at the top. Without any words, I offered it as a blessing to the new home from Source.

Afterwards, I shared this experience with my friend, and she invited me to stay for a while longer. I led her family in a brief crystal singing bowl circle. As a token of appreciation, her parents, visiting from India, invited me to speak with their Punditji, Mahesh Bhai. Since he had stayed up all night to celebrate the full moon, we were able to connect with him through online messaging.

During our conversation Mahesh Bhai spoke of a star symbol on my right palm. It was a voice conversation, so we couldn't see each other nor could I see the star on my palm he was referring to. I didn't know what he was looking at. After taking a photo of my palm and sending it to him, he drew a circle around the star, describing it as a chakra symbol.

It was almost too subtle to notice, but with his help we could see it clearly. He went on to say that I possessed great power, but had not yet achieved control over my mind. He predicted that it could take two decades for me to reach my full potential, and that I would live a fulfilled life. He predicted another life-threatening event that same year, implying another near-death or spiritually transformative experience, and then he spoke openly about my divorce.

Although his belief system did not usually support

divorce, he advised me that since it was happening to me, to let it play out. It was meant to happen. He also told me that after returning to embodiment from my precious near-death experience, I possessed "Shakti" energy, which commonly refers to the creative energy of the universe. He called me a "Super Soul." I was honored, though I still don't know what that means.

I was amazed by Mahesh Bhai's powerful message, and I couldn't believe he was talking about me. My awe turned to surprise when he asked me to read him. I didn't think I was ready; my messages came through when they were meant to, not on command.

However, I wanted to return the favor. I told my friend to tell him that I would send energy through my hands to him. I called in the energy "whoosh" and began sending. It flowed effortlessly at first, until it suddenly stopped.

As I sent the energy to the Punditji on the other side of the world, I suddenly felt a blockage. It was like an unseen garage door dropped down in front of me, preventing the flow.

Miraculously, even though he couldn't see me, Mahesh Bhai felt the block the exact moment it happened. Despite the language barrier, he spoke in Hindi at that very moment, stating:

"She is powerful but quite blocked. She needs clearing and protection."

I knew he was right. I scheduled a healing session for the next day.

The following day, I connected with my dear friend and renowned Pranic healer, Lorna Christensen, seeking her expertise for an energy clearing. Lorna has been my go-to healer whenever I sense the need to cleanse my energy. I listened to music on my end while she worked on me remotely, skillfully conducting energy healing. Using a powerful large crystal to amplify the process, she focused on severing energetic ties connected to my ex-husband. As I laid down and relaxed during the session, I felt a sharp and significant pain in my root chakra. It was intense enough that I had to consciously breathe through it.

After the session, she spoke first, explaining that a significant part of her work had been clearing energy blocks associated with my ex-husband from my root chakra. In that instant, I discerned the origin of the intense pain. She shared with me about the subtle energy connections that unknowingly bind us to others. This energy, sometimes unintentionally connected, was still affecting me. The process of severing those ties and reclaiming some of my energetic power proved to be an empowering experience.

Days later, I received a gift in the mail from Mahesh Bhai. He had mailed me a beautiful token of protection, which I carried with me for the next few months as I battled an unknown, severe respiratory illness. Months later, the amulet disappeared without a trace. I believe it protected me when I came down with the mysterious respiratory illness. When it left, a new teacher and protector entered my life.

Sergan, an astrologer on the other side of the world, reached out to me after he heard an interview about my NDE. He emailed me to tell me how much he resonated with my story. Having studied multiple near-death experiences, he had much to share about the similarities he saw between my journey and that of others. He wrote of my healing hands and how I may have been unconsciously sending healing to clients through the crystal singing bowls. He knew things about my life that were absolutely mesmerizing. Reading my chart, he also spoke of my early life being guided by a partner who held characteristics of a "poison Leo heart," whom I assume to be my ex-husband. In future messages, he gave messages of hope, mentioning that my connection to Source would be strengthened upon meeting my soulmate, as was also clearly indicated in my chart.

I appreciated how Sergan's support arrived at the right time. In gratitude for his insight, and with his permission, I sent him healing energy through my hands. I used classical music and the crystal singing bowls to send him distant healing. Though I hadn't informed him about the timing of when I had sent the energy, and even though he was miles away, he wrote to me instantly, evidently sensing the energy.

He expressed admiration, writing: "*Your healing skills are truly exceptional. Only someone who has had direct contact with the Ascended Masters could achieve such palpable healing.*"

Sergan would continue to send messages. They were unexpected and always appreciated, as they would arrive out of the blue, offering encouragement and acknowledgment of what I was going through. We shared resources and emailed back and forth about spiritual matters in the world. He even provided guidance for my crystal singing bowl practice.

As time went on, I started sharing with larger audiences and hosting spiritual retreats. In January 2022, during my first co-hosted spiritual retreat in Hawaii, another experience unfolded. Meticulously organized, the retreat featured twelve carefully selected participants from the interconnected circles of myself and co-facilitator LeeYen Anderson.

LeeYen and I had been called to work together months before, and always knew we had a strong spiritual connection. We've known each other for a short time in this lifetime, but have been through many previous lifetimes together. We are united by a shared mission on this planet, and it's remarkable to observe that a significant number of our retreat participants seem to be on the same path. As will be explored in later chapters, our retreats have been witness to pure magic— transformative, life-changing experiences that defy explanation, yet radiate with the most beautiful, loving energy.

Within the structure of the retreat, LeeYen and I held private sessions. In these sessions, I conducted healing sessions and offered insights into my spiritual process, which I call "Journeys." This term best describes the experience of venturing into different realms and encountering light beings, angels, animal guides, and messages from a higher Presence. Many describe this feeling as. Being "lifted up," transcending to realms of unimaginable love and insight.

Anela, one of the retreat participants, came forward on the first day with a palpable spiritual fullness. From our initial meeting, I sensed an undeniable connection to her soul. Anela embodied the wisdom and spiritual practices rooted in Hawaiian culture, drawing from a childhood tradition passed down from her ancestral line. Her connection to the Earth and reverence for our ancestors became evident as she guided us in reciting prayers and making offerings at sacred land sites. She guided us through Hawaiian Sun Salutations, weaving in the wisdom passed down by the ancestors who once walked the land. Before stepping onto any land in Hawaii, she led us in prayers of gratitude and serenity while asking permission from the land guardians, ancestors and spirits to be in the space.

The moment she settled in for our session, I could distinctly feel the dynamic flow of energy wrapping around me and linking us together. As Anela shared her visions with me, I felt lifted up and found that I could see the *same visions* she was describing to me. It was an emotional experience, and I found myself crying in gratitude next to her.

In one shared vision, we witnessed light beings from different realms who showed us the creation of Earth. So much care and intentionality was put into our world! We were created in love, in celebration! So much so that the light worlds from which we come celebrate our journey on this planet. In addition, I clearly saw that powerful and beloved light beings walk the Earth among us, as part of the plan for expansion and spiritual evolution. We both saw the creation of the earth and the celebrations and honor that are held for us in other realms of light. Statues, celebrations and loving prayers. All meant to assist us in holding the balance for the light from which we come.

Anela and I were shown through these visions that everything that happens is part of a greater design. We have free will, of course, but we are *all* part of the plan. The light celebrates our journeys and pays homage to the difficulty that we have experienced in our spiritual evolution. A message from my NDE came back in that moment: *The light never leaves us; it is with us always.*

We may forget how to access it, but even then we are more powerful than we know. We are not limited to our human constructs and can create Heaven on Earth. It is exactly what we came here to do. This is why I'm so deeply committed to my work, which revolves around channeling this creative energy to bring Heaven to Earth.

Everything in the history of time has led to this moment. We are being uplifted and celebrated. We are continually supported by Source, and the old mindset perpetuated by humankind is being dissolved and reset. We are raising our vibration, as we are receiving more assistance. We are becoming more and more empowered by facing our shadows. When we look at these shadows, we gain insight and wisdom that allow us to expand our consciousness and evolve. We are being guided to release all that no longer serves us to step into our power.

✳ ✳ ✳

Exploring Breathwork

1. **Create a Sacred Space:** Find a quiet and comfortable place where you won't be disturbed. This space can be indoors or outdoors, as long as you feel safe and relaxed there. Consider using soft lighting, candles, or diffuse oils.

2. **Comfortable Seated or Lying Position:** Choose a position that allows you to relax and breathe deeply. If you're lying down, use a yoga mat or comfortable surface. Make sure you're warm enough and have a blanket nearby if needed.

3. **Mindful Breathing:** Begin with a few minutes of mindful breathing. Close your eyes and focus on your breath. Inhale deeply through your nose, allowing your abdomen to rise, and exhale fully through your mouth, letting go of tension with each breath. Allow the exhale to be twice as long as the inhale. Use an essential oil like Gratitude or Release to enhance this experience.

4. **Intention Setting:** What insights are you seeking? It could be related to your past, a current challenge, or simply a desire for spiritual connection and growth.

5. **Deep Breathing:** Begin the active breathing process. Inhale deeply and rapidly through your nose, filling your lungs as much as possible, and then exhale forcefully through your mouth. Continue this pattern without pausing between inhalations and exhalations. Do this for ten breaths and take a break for about thirty seconds. Experiment with holding the breath during the breaks, or tensing every muscle in your body before relaxing and beginning the process again.

6. Let Go of Control: As you continue the rapid breathing, surrender to the process. Let go of any expectations or preconceived notions. Allow your body and breath to guide you. You may notice sensations in your body, emotions surfacing, or even vivid images. If emotions arise, allow them to flow without judgment. This is a space for healing and release. Keep breathing and trust the process.

7. Visualizations and Insights: Breathwork often leads to vivid visualizations and insights. You might experience memories from your past, encounter symbolic imagery, or even feel a connection to higher realms. Embrace these experiences as opportunities for growth.

8. Integration and Closure: After about 15 minutes of active breathing, slow down your breath and return to a natural rhythm. Spend some time in stillness, reflecting on your experience. Consider what you've learned or felt during the session.

9. Journal Your Experience: Open your journal and write down everything you can remember from your Holotropic Breathwork session. Include any sensations, emotions, images, or insights that come up. Don't worry about grammar or structure; this is a personal reflection. Take some time to consider the insights and emotions you encountered during your session. What do they mean to you? How might they relate to your life, challenges, or desires? Consider the symbolic nature of any imagery.

10. Loving Action Steps: Based on your reflections, identify any action steps or changes you'd like to make in your life. Are there patterns or beliefs you'd like to release? Are there new directions or goals you'd like to pursue?

11. Close Your Session: Conclude your Holotropic Breathwork session by expressing gratitude for the experience and any insights gained. Take a few deep breaths to ground yourself in the present moment.

CHAPTER 10

As Above, So Below:
Bringing Heaven to Earth

Choosing love over fear turns life's challenges into
moments of paradise, making heaven on earth a reality.

O N THE other side, I heard this message:
"We create our reality through our thoughts."

Could the shared vision from Hawaii become reality? Does every life experience serve as an opportunity for spiritual growth? What if in this classroom on this planet, we are *meant to create Heaven on Earth?* If so, how does it work and how do we do it?

Imagine a world where we live in harmony and love, free from war and conflict, lifting each other up in the light and freeing one another from the shackles of shame and fear. What if our mission is to bear the torch for those still trapped in darkness and apprehension? By embracing our life experience, including the challenging times, we evolve into beings of spiritual might. As we consider these possibilities, let's reflect on how even our experience of the pandemic lockdown fits into this broader vision.

Thinking back on the pandemic, imagine it served a greater purpose — giving Mother Earth a much-needed rest. While we were inside, the planet seemed to rise in vibration, and priorities began to shift quickly. Individuals began questioning their lives, making changes, and embarking on new beginnings. The collective shadow that emerged during that time served as a catalyst for many to discover a fresh calling. Many found more of themselves in an "inner space" because of the lockdown.

Perhaps this was a first step in bringing Heaven to Earth. Perhaps we needed to be brought back into ourselves and given the opportunity to make a *choice*. We needed to take that step back to move forward into our power. Whatever the case, it seemed to come parallel to the healing of the planet.

Lockdown brought Mother Earth a stilling, which in turn reduced pollution and gave her the space to heal, vibrate at a higher frequency, and grow anew. We came across news stories detailing the recovery of animal populations, and local hotels and businesses, left untended, soon succumbed to the rapid overgrowth of plants. Where we lived, people were not on the streets. There was minimal traffic, and business activities were sparse. The world was eerily quiet.

Among my clients, a notable shift happened as many began seeing others on an energetic level. There was a magnetic pull towards certain individuals, even though the reasons remained unclear. I attribute this phenomenon to the development of our ability to recognize the light within others. I believe that the lockdown brought new intuitive gifts for many.

During this time, new clients came to me seeking guidance on navigating their newfound intuitive abilities. Some reported leaving their bodies during sleep and receiving messages of hope on the other side, while others started having visions and angelic messages. Was it mere coincidence, a stress response, or were we finally quieting our minds enough to hear the wisdom of higher consciousness?

My clients also reported observed more positive situations and people moving into their lives. In some cases, they made the choice to distance themselves from those who depleted their energy. Other times, these energies naturally moved out of their lives by chance, and communication became less frequent.

I used to refer to this phenomenon as the "Covid Cleanse," but now view it more as a "Conscious Cleanse." Conscious Cleansing is something I see as a reward for stepping into a higher frequency life experience, moving further into love and expansion. It is another way to witness the Law of Balance as we clear negative energies from our lives, which allows us to draw in more light, like-minded communities, guides, and healers.

Spiritual Elevation and Collective Awakening

Our collective ascension seems to be directly related to the increased frequency of our planet. The examination of the Earth's frequency through the Schumann Resonance is notable, and provides tangible evidence that the Earth's vibrational patterns have undergone measurable shifts. The Schumann Resonance refers to the resonant frequency of the Earth's ionosphere, primarily in the extremely low-frequency range. Named after physicist Winfried Otto Schumann, the primary frequency is around 7.83 Hz. This resonance fluctuates and can be influenced by lightning discharges, solar flares, and various Earth-related factors. Recent observations have documented instances where the Schumann Resonance has spiked well beyond usual levels, reaching frequencies as high as 36+ Hz.

Many associate the Schumann Resonance with human health, spirituality and consciousness, although scientific consensus on such effects seems limited. The resonance provides a background frequency that has been studied for its potential connections to various natural phenomena. Since the lockdown, the Schumann Resonance has exhibited a gradual and consistent increase, with notable spikes indicating a heightened frequency in the planet's vibrational patterns over time.

With this in mind, it is my belief that the planet has also elevated our frequency, aligning us to a level that brings us closer to the vibration of higher consciousness. Our spiritual bodies *chose and orchestrated* this experience and it had to happen when it did. Now is the time of great awakening.

On December 21, 2021 I received a message from Source suggesting that collectively, we chose to move into a golden age that will bring more light to us all. What does this mean?

It means we're letting go of the negativity that has held us back in the patterns of spiritual evolution for a long time. Now, we're breaking free from limitations and can use that freedom to create positive change worldwide. I truly believe that if we choose positivity and embrace it fully, we can make the world better using tools like music, vibration, light, art, writing, sound, and creative uplifting methods. We might even be able to access parts of the brain that have laid dormant until now.

Everyone on the planet has a choice to join in. For those who choose accept the call, use this book as a resource. Complete the exercises to enhance the connection to your God Presence so that your presence can tell you how to bring more light to the world. May you find more beauty, connection, and love in your life as a result. As you build in these daily practices to change your mindset and spiritual energy, you will be amazed at the shifts you see in your life!

The Golden Age is upon us. The pandemic could even be seen as the catalyst that boosted our spiritual vibrations to a new level. It brought forth the shadow for us to look at, such that our spiritual renewal has sometimes felt overshadowed by the dark side of human nature. Yet we can learn to peel that back to see what's happening beneath the surface. The light cannot shine without first illuminating that which is in the shadows. Here's a small exercise that may show you if the shift has begun for you. I call it "Reflections on the Conscious Cleanse":

Sit back and think for a moment about the energies that surround you in your day-to-day life. Take note of the 3-5 people who are closest to you now. Next, take your memory back to 2019. Have your social circles shifted since the pandemic? Consider the energies influencing your life — what fosters a deeper spiritual consciousness? Are the individuals surrounding you now more aligned with your spiritual path?

When I think back to the months leading up to the pandemic, I clearly see the magic of the events that lined up in my life. With the connection to IANDS, the new spiritual teachers who arrived in my life and messages that flowed, I started to believe more.

When I reflect on it now, it's clear that there was something greater at play. It was as if the universe was allowing me to move through things to support others better. I had the wisdom from my near-death experience to provide hope for those who need more of it in their lives.

Releasing the timeline has been a major part of accepting what is. We are all on our own timelines: a continuum based on the personal life experiences and choices we make. We are awakening collectively, but also individually. We are needed right now to build a new world.

Some may think, *"I don't have the reserves or time for this. I have lost hope and cannot maintain the energy it takes to right the wrongs of the world."* While we may not alter the world as a whole, we have the ability to modify our responses to worldly situations that directly affect us, a task that demands significantly less energy. Start small, by calling in your higher self, meditating daily and learning to consciously replace negative thoughts with positive thoughts. As you practice, the circumstances in your life will guide you to find the next practice. The energy spent doing this is worthwhile because it will shift your life to a higher vibration quickly.

We can bring Heaven to Earth by spreading our individual light into the world. We can create more unity, instead of division. We can reject the story. We can create a new story built from love and lifting each other up. We can receive and give *love instead of fear*. Imagine that world.

Loving actions over time enhance our ability to create a positive upward trajectory in our lives and the lives of others. The ripple effect of positivity is too powerful to measure and will be wonderful when we come together to create it.

Once we begin to take action to create the life of our dreams, we recognize our innate power to collaborate directly with Source, and that will elevate us even more on a spiritual level. Others will see this light and want to be nearer to us. They will want to know the secrets of living in the light.

We will begin working on a level that we never knew was possible. Our adoration and communication with our own God Presence allows us to join unseen spiritual forces of light that will help pull us out of darkness, fear and isolation.

It will not be hard. It will not be draining. It will be uplifting, magnificent, energizing! We will find joy in witnessing the awakening of others and will then unlock gifts in ourselves as we work. This is *truly living.*

Here's a visualization practice:

Take a moment now to reflect on your unique gifts. As you do this, see a powerful loving light surrounding you. Recognize the good that you have created through your gifts. Allow this light to grow as you see all of the love that you have given to the world: every good deed coming back to you, multiplied. Invite your God Presence to bring more of this energy into your life. Invite your God Presence to stay with you, magnifying your purpose with every breath you take.

Reflecting on the People in Your Spiritual Journey

Step 1: Sitting and Setting

Find a quiet and peaceful space where you won't be disturbed. Sit comfortably with your spine straight and your hands resting on your lap.

Step 2: Setting Intentions

Take a few deep breaths to center yourself. As someone who believes in the power of spiritual growth and transformation, set your intention for this exercise, such as, "My intention is to reflect upon people in my life who have been significant for my spiritual journey."

Step 3: Reflections on Your Spiritual Connections

Close your eyes and begin to reflect on the individuals who have played a significant role in your spiritual journey. Think about three to five people who have been close to you at some point in your life and have been supportive guides for you on your spiritual path. Consider how they have influenced your growth, provided support, or inspired you to embrace your gifts.

Step 4: Visualize the Loving Light

Visualize a golden, loving light around you. See this light expand to represent the collective support you've received from these people and your spiritual guides, healers and other light beings. Feel warmth and gratitude emanating from this light as it symbolizes the love and connection you share with these spiritual companions.

Step 5: Connect with Your Higher Self

- Imagine a golden ball of light above your head, representing your higher self. Imagine a golden ray of sparkling light flowing from your higher self into your heart.
- As you reflect on the people who have been part of your spiritual journey, consider how their presence has helped you connect more deeply with your higher self. See their wisdom and love adding to the golden ray from your higher self. See your heart growing like an expanding golden sun.

Step 6: Gratitude and Blessing

- Take a moment to express gratitude for the people who have supported your spiritual growth. Send them thoughts of love and appreciation.
- Know that these connections have been essential in your journey of bringing Heaven to Earth and evolving into a being of spiritual might.

Step 7: Closing Reflection

- Slowly open your eyes, carrying with you a sense of gratitude for the positive energies and connections that have shaped your spiritual path.
- Reflect on how these relationships have brought light and love into your life, aligning you with your higher self and your mission of creating positive change in the world.

CHAPTER 11

Thoughts, Love and Taming Our Consciousness

Harnessing consciousness is the key to crafting a new reality.
By taming thoughts, we unlock the power to
shape a beautiful existence.

ANOTHER message I heard on the other side:
"*Most of what we worry about on Earth doesn't matter.*
Love matters. People matter. How we live matters."

The fears, the worries, the perceived transgressions of our daily lives… they are all distractions. We are not here for that. We are here to lift each other up, bring hope, move people out of fear and help them reconnect with their own power and wisdom.

When I woke up from the coma, this knowledge stayed with me. Even though I felt like coming back to Earth was like being thrown into a pool without knowing how to swim, this "knowing" stayed with me. I taught myself to connect deeply through the shared human experience.

I knew from my experience on the other side that we all

seek *love,* belonging and understanding. From the moment I awoke, I made it a point to let people know that *they matter.* No matter how small the act, uplifting each other is part of our purpose.

This is what led to my spiritual coaching business. Like others who are here to assist, I help people understand what is happening and how to use their intuition to help the world. Through this, we will see healing and connection beyond what we ever thought possible. We will reach a point where we can never even conceive of hurting another human. This will be when we attain true freedom.

My first lesson in my spiritual coaching career was to release expectations of what would come through for my clients, as I could never predict it. I surrendered to the wisdom that each person has the knowledge they seek, through the connection they have with their Presence. The first step to accessing this is to help people move out of the thinking mind into a direct connection with their higher self. The next step is to teach them to release negative thoughts through conscious practice in their daily lives. The discernment of thoughts is a practice that I learned through my meditation training at Naropa. This simple practice has the power to change lives. After all, our thoughts create our reality and thus we can use them to create a more positive reality.

Have you ever encountered a challenging situation, finding yourself spiraling into fears and negative stories instead of releasing shame, blame and control and loving yourself through it? Perhaps it was the frustration of witnessing a good job turn sour, or being in a relationship that slowly chipped away at self-love, leaving you feeling trapped? Such situations often start with seemingly small issues, which we might brush off, thinking "it's not that big of a deal."

Yet over time, these experiences can start to weigh on us and negatively impact our well-being. Eventually we may even start to feel trapped and powerless, unable to see a way out of the situation. We might start to believe that this is just how it is, that we have no control over our reality. But the truth is that we always have a choice.

Once the realization hits that your situation is no longer serving your greater good, you can choose to take control of your thoughts to shift your life towards a more positive outcome. Does this mean we can change the situation by thinking positively? Not entirely, but by seeing the gifts in the situation, we can integrate the situation more quickly and new paths emerge to take us into a different reality. By shifting thoughts we change our neurological patterns, which opens our minds to new possibilities and opportunities. In the next section, we will explore practical strategies for shifting your mindset and taking control of your thoughts, so that you can start to create a new, more desirable reality.

Navigating Change: Positively Shaping Your Reality

Let's first address the danger of negative thoughts. As situations emerge, we may start to share discontentment with others, becoming more immersed in the story we create to make sense of it. The more we repeat it, the more the story seems to gain validation as we give it more precious emotional energy. We may even convince ourselves that we aren't worthy of anything better, or that we are always the victim stuck in a repetitive pattern. Where attention goes, energy flows!

A dangerous cycle can take hold when we perceive our life experiences as happening "to" us instead of "for" us. This mentality creates the illusion that we lack free will. It can lead to becoming enslaved by our human interpretation of the world, fostering isolation, darkness, and hopelessness. We forget that our thinking is not "right." It's a narrative for which we view the world. It is a distraction from our light. After all, how can one expect perfection in an imperfect place? True perfection resides only on the other side.

Thankfully, there are ways to resolve this through the practice of meditation, daily affirmations, and simple mental training. We can easily learn to replace negative thoughts with positive ones. In the end of chapter exercise, we will explore how to use these tools to create a more positive reality.

One of the simplest practices to master is letting go of negative thoughts *every time they arise*. Thoughts don't stop, but we can train ourselves to manage their direction. Instead of giving our precious energy to negativity, we can choose to focus on gratitude and compassion, thus training our minds to see more of what we want in life. It's a practice that can change our lives, one thought at a time.

❋ ❋ ❋

Thought Discernment Meditation:
A Journey into Mindful Awareness

Step 1: Setting
Locate a quiet space where you won't be disturbed. Create an environment that fosters tranquility, perhaps with soft lighting, by diffusing oils or with soothing sounds. Sit in a comfortable chair or lie down on your back. Ensure that your body is relaxed and warm, and that you won't be interrupted during the meditation.

Step 2: Centering Breath
Gently close your eyes to bring your focus inward. Inhale slowly and deeply through your nose, allowing your lungs to fill with fresh air. When you have taken a full breath, breathe in a little more to "top it off." Hold the breath for a moment before exhaling slowly through your mouth. Repeat this a few times to settle.

Step 3: Observing Your Thoughts
- Visualize Passing Clouds: Envision your mind as an expansive sky, creating more and more space with each outbreath. As thoughts arise, picture them as clouds moving away from you. Let each outbreath carry more clouds of thoughts away from your mind. Feel the spaciousness in your mind.
- Non-Attachment: Practice observing your thoughts without attachment or judgment. Let them come and go, labeling them as thoughts and acknowledging their presence without dwelling on them.

Step 4: Thought Discernment
- If you have a recurring thought, give it a moment of attention,

asking yourself, "Does this thought serve me positively? Is it aligned with love and empowerment?"

- Letting Go: If the thought doesn't align with love and positive energy, replace it with three thoughts that shift it, or are the opposite of the negative thought. Visualize these additional positive thought clouds emerging in the vast sky of your mind, growing larger than the initial negative thought cloud. Then consciously release them all, letting them drift away into the sky. Notice how you feel lighter from this.

Step 5: Reflection

- *Journaling:* After the meditation, take a few moments to open your eyes. Have a journal ready to capture your reflections.
- *Note Shifts in Awareness:* Record any shifts in your awareness during the meditation. Pay attention to how it felt to observe your thoughts without attachment.
- *Explore Discernment Experience:* Reflect on the discernment process. Did certain thoughts surprise you? How did it feel to consciously choose thoughts aligned with love and positivity?

CHAPTER 12

The Journey Through Everyday Discoveries

"The real voyage of discovery consists not in seeking
new landscapes, but in having new eyes."
— MARCEL PROUST

HAVE you ever noticed that teachers tend to show up in our lives at just the right moment? This is not mere co-incidence; it's by design. This is why it's not a surprise that when Lilia first reached out to me, it was after I had specifically asked for guidance from Source. When I made my request to the universe, the response came powerfully and within days.

By September 2019, I had not only connected with Lilia, but I also received: an invitation to the IANDS Conference; a message from Jane about the future of my life; three power-ful spiritual books to guide me on my path forward; a team of spiritual teachers and a beautiful community; and a revisita-tion by an Ascended Master and multiple beings of light. It was as if, in responding to the call to step into my life's path, a whole army of Earth angels and light beings showed up to support me. All this happened in such a short span of time that it left me feeling both amazed and grateful. It was clear that the universe was working to bring me exactly what I needed, exactly when I needed it.

We can receive Source messages through many channels, through friends, colleagues, spiritual teachers, strangers, nature, songs, poetry, and even the words of children. Anything in your world can be a message. When you open your awareness to it, you can hear messages in everything. Over time, I have become more attuned to these messages and learned to decipher them. Children can be particularly adept at hearing Source messages, and listening to their stories can reveal profound wisdom.

As a young mother, I would cuddle with my children before bed and feel the presence of Source within them. I would actively send love to surround and protect them, teaching them the ability to work with energy. Through my love and prayers, I saw the love reflected in their eyes and felt a deep connection. My children became my living teachers, reminding me of the beauty and wonder of life. As they grew, they brought countless messages and taught me to remember the divinity in all things. Not knowing what they were saying, they even shared stories about their past lives. This served as validation for me of the messages I had received on the other side, affirming the idea that we have been here before.

One time, while my two-year-old son was taking a bath, he looked straight into my eyes and asked, "Mommy, do you remember when I was your dad and I took care of *you*?" Another time, my two-year-old daughter asked me if I remembered when she died from a snake bite in her stomach in the "North Desert."

When my oldest was six, she shared that she could leave her body while she slept and fly over everyone in the house. She checked on us as we slept before she traveled to other worlds. These were not just the imaginations of little ones. They are real reminders of our human potential and the intentionality of our lives together.

However, as my children transitioned into their teenage years, the dynamic shifted, and the role of a parent became an intricate dance. It became less of a spiritual experience and more of a practice of mastery in holding loving space. It has been a challenge to remain balanced while navigating life situations that arise, all without projecting my own unresolved wounding onto their experiences.

A wise man once said that the true challenge in his Zen mastery was to remain in the present moment as a parent. This couldn't be more true. As children grow and find themselves, they push boundaries so they can individuate, often turning anger into the fuel for independence. This growth phase involves appreciating the light in them as they evolve, and pulling back to allow them to find their way. I try to remember that no one knows what is better for them than their own higher presence. My role as a parent is to guide them in uncovering the truth within, while also establishing boundaries for safety and helping them see that everything happens for a reason.

Parenting is a beautiful journey filled with wonder and challenges that foster growth. Throughout it, I'm learning to release the need for control and let go of expectations, fears, and the desire for control. While I'm always there for them with support and guidance, it's a practice to surrender to the wisdom that Source is guiding them just as much as Source has guided me. They are on their unique spiritual path. Reflecting on my life, I realize that, just as my parents could only do so much for my spiritual evolution, I, too, have limitations in influencing them on their spiritual path.

As my children adjusted to a new life beyond the comfort of our once intact family, I found parallels between their lives and my own teenage years. As a teen I also navigated an unfamiliar life while recovering from my head injury. Like them, I craved normalcy even if it meant ignoring parts of myself to fit in. My wish for them is to embrace who they are, accept their unique journey, and recognize the special qualities they bring to the world.

The pace for this upcoming generation is remarkably accelerated. What took me years to grasp, they seem to absorb much earlier. My son, entering adulthood, exemplifies this. He comprehends universal intricacies that surpass my own understanding. He operates on a spiritual level akin to individuals who have dedicated years, even decades, to their spiritual work.

My hope is that I supported this spiritual expansion in them when I embraced the nurturing parenting inspired by my mother's family. My mother comes from a family of teachers, including my grandmother Ida, a school principal who dedicated her life to teaching because of her deep love for children. Drawing on generations of wisdom and influenced by the teaching methods in my children's schools (Montessori), I combined natural consequences, conversations, love and logic. This nurtured and supported them both emotionally and spiritually.

It is a shift away from the 'children should be neither seen nor heard' mentality. However, this approach feels right to me. It echoes lessons from my Near Death Experience: lead through love and embrace our differences. Our differences are what make us valuable to the world. This mentality mirrored what I experienced in my personal life as I returned to myself. By creating healthy boundaries and staying true to myself, I could more easily expand my light to share with my children and with the world.

I encountered numerous challenges and made mistakes while exploring different approaches for our new family dynamic. In my struggles, I sought counseling and parental coaching for myself and the kids. This helped us learn together. It was difficult as as a single mother, especially when compounded with the financial struggles of divorce.

There were moments when things felt never-ending and even hopeless. Navigating financial struggles in the wake of my ex-husband's evasive financial maneuvers presented its own set of trials. I found solace in my tried-and-true practice: I confronted negative thoughts, stayed committed to my spiritual practice, sought support from my community, addressed aspects of myself that needed attention, and looked for signs that I was on the right path. I stayed dedicated to my spiritual path. Daily meditation, reading spiritual books and prayer gave me the tools to see that even in the face of adversity, inner peace was possible.

This time of my life was the most vulnerable, beautiful, raw opportunity to move through human discord. I learned how to lovingly stand up for my relationship with my children. I learned financial boundaries and autonomy.

Saying no to their requests for after-school activities and fun outings was not an easy thing to do, but I learned to prioritize our financial stability. The financial strain prompted me to find mentors who could help me overcome limiting beliefs surrounding money. I offered session trades, offering sessions in return for other forms of expertise, enabling me to confront my fears related to finances. Through this process, I discovered new avenues to receive abundance and shifted away from the belief that money equaled abundance. I found that abundance comes in different ways, including meaningful connections, personal growth, and the richness of experiences that go beyond mere monetary value.

As I redirected my focus towards personal growth during the divorce experience and sought positivity in every situation, I started attracting more healthy friendships, career opportunities and life experiences. I started working with the art of manifestation and welcomed healthy partnership into my life. (Details on manifesting a healthy romantic partnership will be explored in a later chapter of this book.) Throughout it all, my children saw me transform into a healthier person with more fulfilling relationships. I started to glow with a new light. As I grew, so did they. Our paths of spiritual evolution were intricately intertwined.

Sometimes the hardest part of this is releasing control to a higher power. I accomplished this by continuing to practice daily prayers for help. You can ask the same questions:

"Where would You have me go?"

"What would You have me do?"

"What would You have me say, and to whom?"

Reflecting on these questions brought me comfort and helped me integrate life lessons with the wisdom of my higher self. This, in turn, empowered me to release old lessons, preventing the need to re-experience them. I could consciously shift my perspective and let go of outdated aspects of myself that no longer served my growth.

Your spiritual path will intertwine with your life lessons, and with faith, love, and dedication to personal growth, you will emerge stronger. As you adapt daily practices like meditation, breathwork, sound healing, positive affirmations, therapy, or journaling, you will see the patterns and overarching themes of life. Once you recognize these patterns, you can energetically close off those lessons, freeing yourself from their recurring presence. Once you identify these old versions of you, complete the following exercise to bring full closure. These are tools that can help you acknowledge these lessons as enhancing your gifts to the world. Use the next exercise, called the "Sacred Flame Healing" as a tool for healing past versions of your self and your ancestral line.

Sacred Flame Healing

1. Preparing the Space: Find a quiet, comfortable space. Take a few deep breaths to center yourself.

2. Reflections: Close your eyes and reflect on old wounds or aspects of yourself that need healing. Visualize these aspects with clarity, letting images pop into consciousness briefly.

3. Sacred Flame Invocation: Envision a beautiful, loving flame (e.g., violet flame) consuming these old parts of you, or parts of your ancestral line. Notice the color of the flame that comes through.

4. Transformation: See the flame consume and seal off the old version of yourself or ancestral patterns. Witness the loving energy of the flame transmuting the past into light.

5. Calling Back the Light: Visualize globes of light from those sealed-off aspects flowing back into your current self, enriching your light being. See and feel the healing.

CHAPTER 13

The Power of Prayer for Visions

Prayer is the intentional conversation with the divine,
a powerful force that not only sends out our desires but sets in
motion the forward momentum toward creating them in the world.

I REMEMBER so many nights when all I could do was pray. I asked my higher presence for guidance, hoping beyond hope that my children would move past anger around the divorce and find their way back to balance. I asked my higher presence to take control of our relationships and hold steady with them until they, too were ready. This practice is powerful. If you wish to foster healing in relationships in your life, envision a miniature version of an ascended master — like Jesus — firmly upon their forehead where the third eye is. I then ask that their presence guide them to the light. This transformative practice is inspired by the teachings found in the I AM Discourse books.

As I read spiritual books such as the I AM Discourses more and more, I discovered that messages flowed to me regularly. When I led music and imagery workshops, I saw light anomalies in the room where I was working. They looked like solid light or patterns of light around the people I worked with. I also still saw visions of light beings in different formations around the circle. These new skills spontaneously emerged, revealing the power of prayer in connecting me to a higher consciousness. It became clear to me that through prayer, we can tap into wisdom, guidance, and support beyond our own understanding.

I remember the workshop when I first saw light beings bending over participants, holding healing hands over their bodies. Another day, I saw concentric circles of light beings around everyone. Other days, light figures would appear in rows, wearing a sash and holding a staff, in absolute stillness. The first time this formation came through, I was leading a workshop at a friend's house. There was a mother in the group who had recently tragically lost her young child. We had come together to support and be with her. At the beginning of the session, tall and powerful light beings showed up in perfectly straight, immobile rows. There were hundreds there with us. They were loving, powerful guardians that left me in great reverence.

I wanted to know more about these visions that appeared during my workshops. I also knew that I couldn't find the answer outside of God, so I went directly to the source. I asked God:

"What kind of angels came today, and why did they appear in formation? What do the formations mean?"

These questions ultimately led me to meet Lilia, who heard the call thousands of miles away. God spoke to her and she called me the next day. She has since become a trusted mentor and guiding presence in my life. May this serve as a reminder to you, dear reader, to ask God for answers.

The power of prayer extends beyond merely asking for our desires; it involves opening ourselves to receive the wisdom and guidance of the universe and taking action on that guidance.

This brings to mind another intriguing experience that occurred just before lockdown. During a meditation session with my coach, Emilia Nagy, on a San Diego beach, three tall light beings manifested before us. They stood there gently looking at us, sending love. Behind us, they formed concentric half circles. I saw powerful figures representing the divine masculine, often described as yang energy or the assertive force within the cosmic balance. They were holding space and love for the divine feminine, acknowledging and embracing the nurturing and receptive energy that divine feminine represents. To me, it was clear that the vision marked a shift away from the patriarchal system that has guided the world for so many thousands of years.

I saw a powerful display as they rhythmically drummed and danced vibrant earth dances to celebrate the emergence of the Divine Feminine — an awe-inspiring spectacle. I witnessed the feminine rising powerfully from a fire, symbolizing a restoration of equilibrium, harmonizing the receptive and projective energies within us and in our world. Months later, in a follow-up vision, I saw that we, as a collective, had indeed brought more of the yin and yang energies into harmony within ourselves. This balance allowed more of our soul bodies to move into us and support more light work during this time of global awakening.

After receiving Lilia's call and deciding to attend the IANDS conference, I'd had another encounter, one I haven't yet shared, involving Jesus and Buddha. It happened during a workshop I was leading the day before flying to the East coast for the conference. I played my crystal singing bowls, and my friend Jodi, a powerful energy worker and psychic, was working with me. As Jodi led a meditation, I went inward and was transported to a place of light.

This time, Jesus was sitting across from me on an ornate throne. He was wearing more elaborate, golden clothing than during our first meeting. His presence still radiated unconditional love and acceptance. Buddha stood to his right, adding to the powerful energy in the space.

During this encounter, I noticed that Buddha had a symbol on his forehead. I sensed the symbol had significance, though it would take time to fully understand its meaning. Their visit felt like a validation of my decision to attend the conference, and now I know it was also an omen of a major life change. After all, it was only a few days later when I met my most influential spiritual mentor and received an accurate and powerful psychic reading.

Reflecting on the prayers from that period, it's evident that they significantly accelerated the unfolding events. Things were transpiring at an astonishing pace. While it was not easy by any means, it was a blessing. I was finally rediscovering myself, feeling guided, protected, and supported every step of the way.

A simple prayer request to God set me on a path that seemed destined for me, mirroring the lessons from my Near Death Experience. The swift and effortless flow of events re-inforced the idea that I was on the right path. In the subse-quent days and months, I leaned on my spiritual practices, in-sights from spiritual books, meditation, community, and the conscious choice of love over fear. Despite witnessing every-thing around me changing, I was able to rebuild with a more solid foundation. My frequency rose as I continued to sur-render daily to Source, leading me to more insight in my life and work. I am grateful for the power of prayer and the sup-port of the Universe that helped me navigate this transforma-tive journey.

A Guided Prayer Exercise

1. Set a Sacred Space

Choose a serene and dedicated space for your practice, creat-ing an environment conducive to spiritual connection. Light a can-dle or incense if it enhances the atmosphere.

2. Invoke Divine Presence

Begin with a moment of gratitude, expressing appreciation for the divine presence that surrounds and supports you. Invoke your higher self and welcome a chosen divine being into your sacred space.

3. Express Intentions and Feelings

Share your deepest intentions, emotions, and specific requests with sincerity. Speak from the heart, articulating your desires and seeking guidance or support.

4. Visualize a Sacred Symbol

Enter a meditative state and visualize a radiant sacred symbol that holds personal significance for you. Imagine this symbol glowing with divine energy, representing the presence of higher wisdom and positive forces.

5. Closing with Gratitude

Conclude your prayer with expressions of gratitude. Thank your higher presence and the divine being for their presence and guidance. Express openness to continued connection and insights.

Try this prayer exercise with me and my crystal singing bowls. Visit **www.wellnessmusictherapy.com** to engage in this experience with me and deepen your spiritual connection.

CHAPTER 14

Finding Magic in the Mundane

"The miracle is not to walk on water. The miracle is to walk on the green earth, dwelling deeply in the present moment and feeling truly alive." — THICH NHAT HANH

THIS chapter is dedicated to the art of reading the signs that come to us after we pray. Source is constantly communicating with us, but we don't often hear the call. We might have things happening repeatedly in our lives that seem mundane or unimportant, and that repetition may, in fact, be an important message from the Divine.

Messages can come through colors, animal sightings, messages from friends or spiritual coaches, body sensations, dreams, visions, music lyrics, or a number of other ways. Our job is to recognize the signs and integrate their lessons into our waking world.

Signs evolve over time. When I first started the practice of recognizing them in my daily life, they were simple: repeated numbers, animals, song lyrics, synchronicities, and dreams. While I still see those signs, I've found that when I go inward to lead workshops or in deep meditations, things have become even more magical. In workshops, I see powerful light rays and colors. For example, I'll see a violet ray or call in the violet flame for healing and cleansing. I recognize these rays of color as significant and spiritual. For instance, a golden ray frequently emerges when the intention is to connect with my higher presence. Interestingly, even when I don't explicitly mention it, clients participating in our workshops often report seeing the same color in their visualizations.

I have enjoyed studying the spiritual meaning behind certain colors. I follow the meanings laid out through the research on chakras, as written about by Anodea Judith in her book *Wheels of Life*. The book explores the concept of chakras and provides a comprehensive guide to understanding and working with the energy centers in the body. Her belief is that white and violet represent Source, indigo represents intuition, and blues are signs of unlocking the voice and intuition. Green and pink typically represent heart healing, while yellow connects us with our authentic self and warrior energy. Orange is typically about self-nurturing, and reds are about manifesting, safety, grounding or calling in support from Mother Earth.

If the belief holds true that every life experience is an opportunity to draw closer to Source, we can extend this understanding to recognizing signs during life challenges. After all, "It's not what happens in life, but how you deal with it that matters." In the face of challenges, when we find gratitude within the difficulty, we can open our awareness to actively look for signs to guide us through it.

Here are a few ways to do this.

First, call your higher Presence in to help. Ask for guidance. We have the gift of free will, which means that our God Presence cannot intervene without permission.

After that, it's a process of retraining the mind. Practice releasing the story and finding the small nuggets of joy and gratitude within the situation. Even when it feels impossible to be grateful, this simple act can shift our worlds entirely. As you focus more on joy and gratitude, you will see more things in your life to be grateful for. You are in essence, retraining the brain through this practice.

Start to call in signs through a simple exercise before falling asleep. I call the time between wakefulness and sleep the "in-between", when we can most effectively call upon Source to guide us.

During the "in between" time, think of an event in your life in which you need guidance. Take yourself to that very moment, recalling the feelings, sensations, and images that came to you. Think of a time when you felt this way before. Take time to notice how you feel in your body as you relive this memory.

Then, imagine that you can communicate with yourself at the time of the memory. Ask what it needs from you to be healed. When it responds, imagine that you can fill the memory with everything that it was asking for, even if it doesn't make sense to your logical mind. You can go a step further by imagining different ways of reacting to the situation. Can you see yourself having clearer boundaries in the moment, laughing in the face of adversity or even walking away? How can you shift your response to it in the most loving way?

The in-between state before sleep is a powerful means to learn to connect with Source. It's a great time to imagine visually whatever is needed in that moment, so you can integrate it and move forward in your spiritual expansion. Doing this will help you start to get messages and signs in your waking life.

Here's an example of this from my work with a client. In her session imagery, she received what looked to be a small metal staff. I asked her to find out what the object needed from her and she responded that it needed her to 'Allow.'

From the depth of her soul, she sent energy of "allowing" the object that had been placed in her hands. That is when she saw the staff transform into different types of gold with shades of white. She was left with the message that her light beings were trying to work through her but needed her to "allow" their wisdom to come to her. They invited her to allow them more presence in her life.

In processing this experience with her after, it became apparent that she'd been hiding her spiritual gifts for years. She is now choosing to allow her own magic to move through her and into the work she is meant to bring to others. I gave her several daily exercises and guided meditations to help her anchor her intentions and allow for more of what she wants to create in the world. Soon after, she started seeing more signs in her waking work, like dozens of crows that would come to her daily with the messages of positive manifestation in her life.

Some people receive signs and don't know it. They ask me how they can distinguish between a message from Source and a human thought. There is a simple way to tell. If the message is accompanied by a strong emotion, it is likely a human fear or thought, not a spiritual message. However, if it comes through without an emotional charge with no sense of time or space, it is likely a message from Source.

Also, if you see the same image or animal (or hear the same song lyric) three times, that is another way to know that your higher mind is communicating with you. You can also ask for body signs to validate the message that is coming through.

As an example, you can give the sway test a try. I picked up this method from Jack Canfield, and it's used by other well-known teachers like Martha Beck, possibly originating from Kinesiology. Begin by standing still, closing your eyes, and calling on your higher presence. In this moment, you will notice your body sways when it is in alignment with your higher self. You can then ask to call in only that which is for the greater good and communicate with your higher presence through your body.

Your body will sway differently when demonstrating a "yes" versus a "no." This can help you gain clarity and insight about your path forward. It's important to note that this is not a way to predict the future, but rather a tool for connecting with Source and making choices in alignment with your highest good. Cultivating a daily practice to enhance your connection with Source messages can be a simple yet profound way to live a more authentic and fulfilling life. My personal journey began with meditative and contemplative practices during my training at Naropa and has evolved into a daily habit of asking for guidance, dropping in, and breathing deeply. Even during my lowest moments, I always came back to those simple questions:

"Where would You have me go?"

"What would You have me do?"

"What would You have me say, and to whom?"

Now, my goal is to live each day as if Source is experiencing life through me in my physical body. This allows the signs to flow more freely to me, as I invite God into every experience. If God is present in every moment, then the communication from the Divine is constant! When I'm living for Source and Source *lives through me*, life flows with ease and I feel aligned with my true self. May your own practice bring you closer to your highest self and the divine wisdom that surrounds us all.

✳ ✳ ✳

Connecting with Source Messages Through Body Wisdom

Step 1. Preparation
- Find a quiet and comfortable space where you won't be disturbed.
- Stand with your feet together and close your eyes.
- Take a few deep breaths to center yourself.

Step 2. Connecting with Higher Presence: Call upon your high-er Presence, expressing the intention to receive guidance and insights from Source. Ask to call in only that which is for the greater good.

Step 3. Sway Test for "Yes" and "No": With your eyes closed, ask your body to sway to indicate a "yes" response. Take note of the direction and movement pattern. This is your body's "yes" response.

Step 4. Sway Test for "No": Similarly, ask your body to sway to indicate a "no" response. Observe the distinct movement pattern. This is your body's "no" response.

Step 5. Connecting with Source Messages: Begin asking simple yes/no questions related to guidance or insights you seek. For example, ask, "Is it in my highest good to take on this new client or job?" Pay attention to the swaying response of your body.

Step 6. Validation through Body Signs:
- If you receive a message, further validate it by asking for additional body signs.
- For instance, ask, "Can my body show me a physical sensation or sign to affirm this message?"
- Be attentive to any sensations, tingling, or shifts in energy in your body.

Step 7. Reflect and Journal: After the exercise, open your eyes and take a moment to reflect on the guidance received.

Journal your experiences, noting the questions asked, the body's responses, and any sensations or signs received.

CHAPTER 15

The Call Compels

Follow the signs, take aligned action, and the universe will
reward you with new experiences that elevate your life.

OVER the last several years, I've learned much about the
practice of calling in abundance and the life of my
dreams, but I remember first learning the truths of manifestation when I was in Heaven. I knew that we all have the Divine
ability to co-create the life of our dreams. Source gifted me
with this knowledge so I could come back, live in this truth,
and focus on the messages I am supposed to share.

A beautiful life is within reach for all of us, shaped by the
attention and emotion we invest in it. True manifestation
comes when we pair thoughts with emotion. I discovered
this truth personally when I began practicing a technique
called Life Mapping.

The concept came to me from the book *Life Mapping* by
Beth Abel. A friend of mine found the book, ordered it for
a small group of women, and we met weekly to dive into the

concepts. We poured time and energy into the process, identifying what we wanted in life, including the amount of money we wanted to make, the career we wanted, family life, income, and more. Over the course of six weeks, we created pure magic mapping out our perfect lives. I brought my crystal singing bowls to enhance the circle.

Crystal singing bowls are large bowls made of pure quartz. They sit on a small rubber ring on the floor and are played with suede ringers that create a rich, resonant sound enabling receivers to feel tingles, waves and other sensations. People experience these sound waves in various ways—some feel gentle waves on their skin or vibrations along their spine, while others sense energy pulsating within their chest or abdomen.

Through years of working with clients, I've developed the belief that the water in our bodies and the vibrations within our cells respond to these potent sound waves, realigning themselves toward balance and perfection. The vibrations from these powerful bowls allow people to relax more fully when played, enhancing meditation and spiritual work. They can also be used to take people into altered states of consciousness and brain wave states. Playing two crystal singing bowls that are close in pitch can create binaural beats, which support moving into Theta brainwave states. For a skilled practitioner, these powerful tools allow Source energy to flow more directly into clients. When I work, I invite Source to move through me, then outward through my hands. I can hear the sound of my crystal singing bowls shift as they open the energy of my clients. They have a clearer, more resonant quality of sound and vibrate differently when the energy of the participants is more dense.

I also have enhanced intuitive abilities when I play the crystal singing bowls; they bring in light, color, angels, even the energy of Ascended Masters. They pull out discord and dense energy and call in more light. My clients then feel and hear messages, which is the point of my work: to allow people to experience their own messages and have the visceral experience of receiving light and divine love into their cellular structure.

During the last gathering of our life mapping group, we each presented our maps as I rang the crystal singing bowls. I mapped out a career based around music therapy. My dream was to lead a team of wellness practitioners stemming from my passion for music. I wanted to thrive financially, and I also knew that I was drawn to live in Southern California. In my early thirties, I had only been to Southern California once in my life. I loved the photos I'd see from friends who visited there. It just seemed magical to me.

But the true reason I opted for California was somewhat peculiar. A few weeks before creating the manifestation Life Map, I stumbled upon a geographic map of allergens at my immunologist's office. This map outlined allergens specific to various regions. What intrigued me was that Southern California was the only place in the country where the plants that caused my seasonal allergies didn't thrive.

My heart lifted as I started to entertain visions of Southern California. The idyllic beaches, the prospect of living near the ocean, and the cultural elements that promote spiritual and emotional growth — all these dreams started vividly taking shape in my mind.

Also, I was so plagued by seasonal allergies that I imagined a place where I could stop taking shots and enjoy being outdoors again. We all had a good laugh when I said to the group, "Sounds fun, but there's no way I'd be able to live in SoCal!"

Turns out that joy and laughter were probably what helped the vision to be realized. You see, emotion is the key to positive manifestation. I should have buckled in, because I had no idea *just how quickly* my life was about to change!

Almost as soon as the ink dried on the map, my life took a turn. It was like the universe said, *"Finally! You gave me a direction. I will create this vision with you! Wish granted."*

My husband was offered a job in San Diego *the very next day*; we were living in Southern California within a month. The house sold in about a week. Everything moved quickly. I found a local like-minded community and I started attending blessing circles and meditations, and began group sessions with my crystal singing bowls. It wasn't long before I built a healing business using music therapy and healing sound as the main focus. I was manifesting my map, creating the life I wanted to live.

What was the magic in the process? The weekly map

meetings helped me raise my frequency enough to co-create with Source. The process of bringing attention to my dreams was planting seeds for life change. As they say, "Energy flows where attention goes."

Week by week, I had intentionally mapped a new life. I enhanced this by bringing in my crystal singing bowls: activating my connection to music and increasing my connection with my God-Presence. I sealed this process by focusing on gratitude and joy around these visions of my future.

Looking back, it's so clear. By connecting the power of thought with the power of frequency, emotions, sound and visualization, I became the designer of a beautiful life.

Maintaining a high frequency amidst low vibrational input is crucial for us to co-create with Source. Not everyone can create a weekly life mapping group, but there are other ways one can stay at a high vibration. The first of these is through learning to control thoughts. A simple meditative practice of releasing negative thoughts is the first step to mastering manifestation.

To be clear, it's not that we don't *feel* a negative thought, but that we have the ability to transmute it immediately. How? By noticing it, labeling it, letting it go, and replacing it with a positive thought about the same subject.

This does not stop negative thoughts completely. Rather, it decreases the negative thought patterns over time. It takes daily practice, such as releasing negative thoughts in traffic, at work, when parenting, and every other ordinary or difficult situation that happens. This constant practice helps you re-shape your world. You begin to see more positivity in the world and more proof that you are succeeding in your life goals. Each goal brings more joy, more hope, more possibility. Over time, you are on cloud nine, perhaps not even realizing that you are living in the world you have painstakingly created by becoming more disciplined in your thought process.

Another simple way to add to this technique is to use high frequency modalities such as crystal singing bowls, medita-tion, or essential oils after releasing negative thoughts. As soon as you receive a negative thought, actively release it from the mind. Some people say "Cancel, cancel, delete, delete."

I prefer to send thoughts out of my mind and imagine them being consumed by a violet flame or annihilated by the light. I also sometimes pretend they are being pulled out of my head, then sending them into the light. I even imagine a thought traveling far from my physical form, over the moun-tains or the ocean. I always open a window or door to signify sending out a thought. Since these moments often occur while I'm driving, my kids have come to understand the significance when I crack the car window to let a thought out of my mind.

You can take this practice further by consciously replac-ing the negative thought with an affirmation. You can en-hance the shift even more by breathing in a high frequency, essential oil. Now, we are taking a page from the book of posi-tive psychology. We are retraining our brain. By associating a positive thought with an affirmation, we anchor that positive thought in the limbic brain. When using an high quality, Absolute Pure essential oil, we have the potential to move that oil through the neuron into the amygdala. This can greatly affect the limbic brain to shift emotions and can work within thirty seconds. I have seen this technique work on so many levels in sessions, supporting people with everything from releasing past trauma to regaining control of their lives.

One client sought my assistance because she was struggling with grief and hadn't been able to release it. She claimed she had not been able to cry for over two years. In our session, I introduced her to essential oils, inviting her to smell several bottles before the session. Sensing her need for release, I handed her an empty oil bottle of an oil called Release, which still had a trace amount in the bottle, but not enough for a full drop.

As she sniffed the bottle of Release, tears welled up in her eyes. As she inhaled, tears flowed, unlocking emotions long held captive. Swiftly, we moved to a healing mat, where I applied another oil to her wrists and had her hold the empty bottle of Release under her nose. I rang a crystal singing bowl on her abdomen, facilitating a cathartic release. This powerful moment underscores the ability of essential oils to shift emotions and clear what the body holds, providing a simple avenue for emotional healing.

To raise your vibration and bring more positivity into your life, try this simple exercise. Breathe an Absolute Pure essential oil such as Release or Joy as you recite positive affirmations daily. Try also exploring various techniques like breathwork, guided imagery, Reiki, different types of meditation, somatic experiencing methods, and other energy-related practices. An approach that has personally helped me substantially is visualization. Visualizing positive outcomes and focusing on possibilities helps you to maintain a high vibration and let go of negative thoughts. My professional work focuses on this: teaching people how to incorporate these diverse modalities into their lives for an overall higher vibrational state.

Many of us take the long road to spiritual manifestation and connectedness because we falsely believe our human selves can control more of our life situations and outcomes than we actually can. Yes, we have freedom of choice and autonomy, which does change outcomes and life paths. But surrendering to the truth that a higher power guides our lives is what truly enables the fast track to spiritual growth. This means releasing the desire to manage life and trust that everything is happening for a reason.

It's disheartening to see friends and colleagues lose themselves to situations beyond their control. Many find themselves in battles where they end up sacrificing parts of their lives and personalities to navigate challenging circumstances. What they don't realize is that there is a faster way... a more fluid, healing, fun, and loving way.

What is the way? To release it. Surrender the situation to our God Presence. Our God Presence is always in action for our greater good. It is the disconnection with this Presence that leads to difficulty in life. As humans we *have great power* in creating our existence, but it is only through direct collaboration with our higher presence that we get there.

When stress and overwhelm start to take hold, I have a release practice that I turn to. I first allow myself to *feel* the discomfort fully. I sit with it, allow it to exist and ask my higher presence take the situation from me. I ask for insight:

"What is the discomfort trying to tell me? What does it want me to know?"

When the answer comes, no matter what it is, I funnel that *thing or* feeling into the discomfort. If it doesn't know what it wants, I send confusion in. When it manifests as fear, I send it my fear. If it seeks acceptance, I flood it with acceptance. After going through this process, I will ask again: "What do you need?" When it eventually requests the need for love or light, I send light and know that this marks the completion of my healing work. I send love and light and then visualize a spiritual panel of guides and angels pulling the issue from my life. I release all to them, earnestly requesting that they orchestrate the best possible outcome aligned with my highest purpose and for the greater good on Earth.

If I struggle to believe this will happen, I pray for powerful surrender and trust to take hold. I do this because I have come to know that surrendering in faith is the quickest way to clear inner obstructions. Each day, I sit in joy and gratitude and ask Source for guidance, use specific oils to anchor me to my purpose, bring love to my path, align my voice with my purpose, and call in more support from the Divine.

What would have taken me years to work on and release is quickly resolved with the support of Divine love and light. As we call to Source for support, our God Presence moves into action to answer our calls. The call compels, and we can surrender in faith that the call will be answered.

❋ ❋ ❋

Life Mapping Meditation
with Crystal Singing Bowls

Step 1. Setting the Space: Set aside a peaceful and sacred corner for yourself, eliminating distractions to ensure a serene environment.

Step 2. Introduction: Commence with a brief personal reflection, visualizing and mapping out the life you desire. Ring the bowls as you imagine the positive manifestation of your life map.

Step 3. Life Mapping Guidance: Take a few moments to reflect on different facets of your life, such as career, relationships, personal growth, and well-being.

Write down specific goals and desires in each area using your journal or paper.

Step 4. Crystal Singing Bowl Activation: Sink into a meditative state as you settle into a comfortable seated position. Elevate the experience by diffusing oils like Abundance, Build Your Dream, Magnify Your Purpose, or Gratitude. Let the bowls resonate for 3-5 minutes, attuning yourself to the vibrations on your body. Feel the subtle shifts and continue to immerse yourself in the sensations. For added connection, engage in pairs, taking turns receiving the soothing vibrations.

Step 5. Guided Meditation: Enter a meditative state in a comfortable seated position. Close your eyes, take intentional deep breaths, and envision your perfectly manifested life map. Focus on the sensory experiences and the feeling of accomplishment. Deepen the meditation by playing your crystal singing bowls as you explore each element of your life map.

Step 6. Sealing the Intentions: As the meditation concludes, guide yourself to express gratitude for your envisioned future. Play the crystal singing bowls in a harmonious sequence, symbolizing the sealing of your intentions into the universe.

Step 7. Closing: Conclude the session by personally expressing gratitude for your energy and intentions. Revisit your reflections regularly, creating affirmations to manifest your desires more swiftly.

Step 8. Reflection and Journaling: After the meditation, take a moment for personal reflection and express gratitude for your experience. Journal your insights and emotions, capturing the essence of your journey and the intentions you've set.

CHAPTER 16

Manifesting Sacred Partnership

"Love is the foundation of true freedom."
– MARTIN LUTHER KING JR.

THROUGHOUT my life journey, I've embraced the art of co-creation and continued to witness the impact of gratitude and joy in every experience. I used to think that things just happened by luck, but now I understand that I have the power to co-create a beautiful life with Source.

Whenever I read a book on manifesting, I can't help but notice how the messages echo what I heard on the other side. Phrases like "Our thoughts create our reality," "We can co-create with Source," and "We are all here for a reason" resonate. Exploring the realm of manifestation reignites my curiosity, serving as a reminder of what I learned and reinforcing what I've experienced.

Each book seems to hold a different piece of the puzzle, and it's only by reading multiple books that I can gather the pieces and integrate those ideas with the messages I received in Heaven. As mentioned previously, the I AM Discourses by Godfre Ray King and Lotus Ray King have had a significant impact on me. These books explore the realm of unlimited possibilities, guiding readers on how to access a higher reality by establishing a connection with their God Presence.

The teachings within these discourses have been a source of inspiration and insight on my spiritual journey. They also discuss how to pair visions with different emotions to manifest more light in my life. This is how I learned that manifestation gains strength when we unite our emotions with our thoughts. When we embrace new spiritual teachings such as these books, we also learn to release control.

How do I know this works? First through my practice of life mapping in Austin and again when I manifested beautiful partnership in my life. I applied what I learned through books and my spiritual experiences, and found love amidst the isolation and stillness of 2020.

It began when I helped facilitate The Abundance Experience with Jack Canfield, journaling about what I wanted in my romantic world. I had a friend I will call Macy, who was also engaged in manifestation practices at the time, and she invited me to join in creating a Life Love Map just for fun. Unexpectedly, this fun endeavor led me to love, even though I truly didn't expect it. At the time, my primary focus was on self-discovery and learning to love myself.

We spent several days exploring what values, emotional, physical and spiritual desires we both wanted in partnership.

It was a fun practice. Little did we know we were developing tools to amplify the manifestation process.

Inspired by the positive experience I had creating my original life map, I accepted the invitation from Macy. The process was so fun and freeing that it brought back memories of my teenage self. With markers in hand and a bottle of wine, we spent an evening creating each of our maps. We played upbeat music, ordered tasty food, and laughed as we brought our visions to paper. We even took a break to dance at some point. It was an uplifting, hilarious night.

I infused my Manifestation Map with essential oil blends, carefully dropping them onto the paper and outlining the drops with markers. The scent of the oils filled my senses as I began to list all the traits I was looking for in my future partner: from clear communication to financial stability, spiritual alignment, physical fitness and humor. I poured my heart into the process, copying notes I'd taken over the last few weeks in and months prior to this. I filled the paper with ideal characteristics and made a game of even hiding secret words within the oil droplets themselves. I then went back and covered each oil drop with marker. As I finished the map and rolled it up, I felt so happy. I went home and put the rolled map away inside a cabinet, forgetting about it almost completely.

In the weeks that followed, I dedicated myself to personal growth with the guidance of my coach, Emilia, who specializes in helping women heal from past emotional abuse and fosters a focus on self-love. She taught me self-love and journaling techniques, encouraging me to embrace my true self and find my inner power. I decided to focus on "dating" myself. I even gave myself flowers and took myself to a movie.

About two weeks after creating and momentarily forgetting about my life-love map, I slid the plastic ring from a geranium oil bottle onto my finger. In a moment of empowerment, I announced to a few girlfriends that I was *enough*. I no longer needed anyone. I was ready to commit fully to authentic self! This light-hearted gesture symbolized a realization of self-sufficiency and joy within.

After this I was unapologetically me. I loved being me. I shed my inhibitions about living a spiritual life and also embraced living out loud. This conscious movement toward self-love may have actually been another key factor to manifesting partnership.

In a beautiful synchronicity, it turned out Macy, my companion in the mapping exercise, had the key to my perfect match all along. For months, she had been encouraging me to meet her friend Neil, who she described as a kind, spiritual man of great integrity. Despite my reservations about being set up, I couldn't help but be intrigued by the possibility of meeting someone who sounded so wonderful.

The notion of meeting Neil in person surfaced several times between February and April of 2020. I remember her bringing him up on multiple occasions, which led me to question my resistance to the idea. At the time, my concern stemmed from the potential awkwardness it might introduce into our friend group. However, with numerous indications pointing towards meeting him, I found myself wondering, "Could the Universe be sending me a message?"

One thing that I've learned along the way is this: strong reactions, whether positive or negative, hold meaning and can lead to important lessons in life. In other words, resistance is not always resistance. Sometimes, it is a sign guiding us toward something that will change us somehow.

After some thought, I decided to open myself up to the idea of a setup if it felt right on a spiritual level. I thought it might be better if I were to meet him naturally, but with lockdown restrictions in place, I couldn't see how that would happen. I surrendered to the Universe and expressed something along these lines to Macy after she brought him up again: "If the Universe presents it to me, I will accept it as a sign!" Little did I know that simple statement would be the beginning of a magical journey, setting off a series of events that would change my life in a matter of days.

Two weeks after creating the map, and one day after telling Macy I'd accept the set-up if the Universe presented it, I received a notification from Hinge, a dating app. In the weeks leading up to this, I'd scrolled through some profiles of potential matches, but wasn't ready to dive into the dating world just yet. It was a fun distraction, but I didn't take it too seriously. Quarantine had drastically altered the dating scene, and I joked that it felt like we were in the 1800s, with text messages replacing love letters.

That day, the notification on Hinge was from a man named Neil. The name caught my eye. Could this be the Neil my friend had been raving about and trying to set me up with? The Neil that I had felt such strong energy around?

I couldn't help but wonder, "How many fitness trainers could there be in San Diego named Neil?" I decided to respond, asking if he a friend named Macy. To my amazement, it was the same Neil! He and I started messaging right away. While messaging each other, we both texted Macy on the side, seeking more details. She not only helped us connect but also gave him advice in talking with me. Things moved pretty quickly from there and Neil and I planned to meet for a sunset walk at Moonlight Beach the following evening.

I stopped by Macy's house before meeting Neil. We spent the afternoon catching up and chatting about my upcoming first date. With lockdown restrictions in place, Macy's beautiful home became a sanctuary where we hung out when our kids were with their dads. After leaving her house, I drove straight to the beach and kicked off my shoes, walking barefoot across the parking lot.

There he was, standing with the sun setting behind him. Instantly, a sense of calm and safety washed over me, and my heart raced with excitement. We felt an unexplainable spiritual connection that bound us together. Later, Neil confessed that he knew right then and there that we were meant to be. In a delightful synchronicity, I discovered that he, too, had created a manifestation abundance map just a few weeks before we met. It served as a validation of the potency of manifestation and the energetic connection between us.

As we approached each other in the parking lot, he felt the connection, smiled, and playfully asked, "Where did you come from?" Taking his question literally, I answered, "From Macy's hot tub." Later, I realized that he meant it as a metaphor for the serendipitous way we had found each other. We still chuckle whenever we remember that moment.

Our conversations flowed so naturally that first night that we missed the sunset entirely as we walked along the beach. We then moved to the benches overlooking the ocean, talking and enjoying each others energy. It was like we had known each other forever, and yet we were discovering something new and exciting in every moment. Hours passed like minutes, and we chatted until it got cold.

We then moved to his car to watch the waves after it got dark. It was amazing how the world rose to meet us on that magical evening. We were graced to witness the most spectacular display of bioluminescent waves that had come to San Diego in over a decade. We moved to his car to watch the waves light up in a stunning aqua color, casting a mesmerizing glow as they crashed to the shore.

Everything was magnified by a waxing gibbous moon. It was as if we had been transported to another world. We couldn't believe our luck to witness such a rare and beautiful sight on our first date. As we stood there in awe of the natural beauty before us, we both knew that we had also found something special in each other. The glowing waves felt like a sign, a confirmation that we were meant to be together, and that our meeting was no mere coincidence.

Everything was vividly surreal, as if we were in a dream. When it got dark, we watched the waves from the warmth of Neil's car, listening to music as we talked. While sitting there, we discovered we shared the same taste in music, providing a soundtrack for our time together. It felt as though the Universe was orchestrating a special chapter just for the two of us. Even when the officers told us to leave because of the quarantine curfew, we couldn't bring ourselves to part ways. We drove to Del Mar, walking along the deserted streets until we found ourselves at Civic Center Plaza, overlooking the nighttime expanse of the ocean.

It was there, with the salty sea breeze blowing through our hair, that Neil kissed me for the first time. I was overwhelmed by the powerful surge that passed between us. Everything else faded away, leaving only the two of us and the intense connection we shared. He picked me up and kissed me again, and it felt like we were the only people in the world.

Since then, our connection has only deepened. We've experienced moments of pure magic together, seeing visions of our past lives and future. I've seen our soul bodies in visions, and they're identical — the same rainbow outline and pattern of constellations. It's a connection that feels divinely ordained, and we both knew from that very first night that it was unlike anything else we'd ever experienced. We choose every day to show up in the most authentic versions of ourselves for each other. Through our relationship, I've learned what true love looks like. It's a choice and a gift.

Due to the pandemic, Neil found himself furloughed from work and I was working remotely, which allowed us to spend most of our free time together, completely immersed in our sacred connection. Our romance was like a fast-forwarded version of traditional dating. With everything closed there were no distractions, no need for pretense. Without the ability to go out, we danced in the kitchen, and led each other through spiritual journeys. I led him through singing bowl and music journeys, and he led me through movement and breathwork experiences.

In the moments when life got challenging, we came together without judgment, offering beautiful support. Laughter was our soundtrack, echoing late into the night. He valued my uniqueness and I loved that I could be myself with him. He taught me to reconnect to the beauty of nature. From sunset beach walks to lazy days, we embraced all of life and learned as much as we could about each other.

We both believe that every experience in our lives led us to find each other, and that our connection has a sacredness to it. Neil even dubbed it our Utopia. For a while, we kept it to ourselves, affectionately referring to it as "Nellentopia."

It was fascinating to experience a healthy relationship after being in a unhealthy dynamic for so long. It required a significant amount of self-work, and I found that I needed to peel away layers of old pain and trauma like an onion. We used Believe oil together, breathing it in as he cupped it over our noses. We knew how blessed we were and wanted to use the oil as a practice of gratitude.

As time passed, I began to look at my failed marriage more objectively and even took a course with a relationship coach, Emilia Nagy, to unlearn the unhealthy patterns I had developed as a coping mechanism. Despite months of work learning to love myself first, I still had fear of being abandoned. After filing for divorce, and before meeting Neil, I had even avoided deep connections for several months. Meeting Neil inspired me to work through my fears and let go of the patterns that were keeping me stuck.

I remember this transformation happening for me about a year after we'd been dating. Despite meeting with a spiritual coach and therapists, working on myself for months, my body returned to a heightened state of fear and I found myself struggling with the story I told myself. The fear of loss overcame me. One day, I was so wrapped in fear, I spent an entire day trying to clear negative thoughts. That's when I remembered the powerful message from Source that had come to me in my NDE: I needed to surrender to something greater.

I distinctly remember saying to myself, "I trust. I am safe. I surrender this relationship over to to my higher presence. Pass it by light."

A sense of lightness washed over me as I repeated "I AM" statements, expressing my gratitude for guidance. Within hours, my Presence answered the call and all my fears melted away.

A few hours later, Neil and I had a healing conversation about trust and vulnerability. He held space for me through my fears, knowing that they had nothing to do with him, but stemmed from an unhealed wound from my previous relationship. His non-judgmental support allowed my true spiritual self to shine. Authentic living involves allowing all aspects of myself to be present, without hiding any part of who I am.

He, too, let down his guard, and we witnessed each other's vulnerable and spiritual selves. A spiritual vision unfolded as I observed our core beings, revealing a golden energy beneath the parts I had attempted to protect. There was beauty in our imperfections. I experienced a connection with him that I had never felt before with anyone. We healed something in that moment, completing a cycle of healing for both of us.

Through this and many experiences since, we have built what we consider to be a sacred partnership. In letting our real selves show and accepting our imperfect parts, we have learned to face challenges together for genuine growth. Sacred partnerships go beyond surface-level interactions — they involve a shared journey of self-discovery where both partners help each other spiritually. It's not about achieving perfection; rather, it's a journey of exploring everything that emerges in the shadow to find our true light. The power of sacred partnerships is in healing and growing spiritually together, creating a strong and transformative bond.

Sacred partnerships are characterized by significant

synchronicities, indicating a destined connection. These meaningful occurrences started from the beginning — beginning with those iridescent glowing waves, our uncannily similar tastes in music, feeling as though we already knew each other, and even the story of our initial meeting. However, more synchronicities arose on our second date when I found the courage to show him my Conscious Love Map. As he studied the map, there was a moment of pause. He looked deeply into my eyes and said, "I am this man."

Hearing those words from him melted my heart; it was true that Neil embodies every quality I wrote on that map. He delights me at every turn of our relationship, as he embraces his authentic, beautiful, loving, powerful self. Through our openness and honesty, we've built a strong foundation of trust and connection that is the bedrock of sacred partnership.

When limiting beliefs arise in our relationship, Neil and I have even developed our own personal routines to overcome them together. One such practice involves using essential oils, affirmations, and shared breathing. Neil takes a few drops of oil in his palms and draws us close together. He covers his nose with his hands, and I position myself in front of him so the other side of his hands cover my nose. This creates a little aroma tent, and we breathe in the scent together. With each inhalation, we gently affirm to each other that we deserve sacred love and are committed to co-creating a magical life together. The words "I am worthy. I am enough. I believe" serve as our mantra, reinforcing our shared journey towards a fulfilling life. This practice helps us to recenter and realign with our shared values and intentions, strengthening our bond even further.

Upon discovering that Neil had also finished a 21-day Abundance meditation just a few weeks before our meeting, I was struck by the synchronicity. It was the Law of Attraction in action. The universe brought us together. I knew then that our meeting was not a mere coincidence, but a tangible manifestation of our shared desires. As our relationship continues to evolve my beliefs about what is possible in a sacred partnership expands. Every day, I see the magic in our spiritual work and the results with our clients, and I'm so grateful for this life.

Acknowledging the significant influence of the Law of Attraction on our journey, I invite you to explore the possibilities of this principle in your own life. As we conclude this chapter, let's engage in an exercise together — crafting a love map. This visual representation of our aspirations and desires will serve as a potent focal point, attracting the positive energies and manifestations we seek in our lives.

✳ ✳ ✳

Self-Love, Personal Growth, and Collaborative

Love Map for Manifesting Love

Step 1: Embrace Self-Love and Reflection

Engage in self-love practices and activities that bring you joy. Reflect on your true self and find your inner power.

Step 2: Journaling and Personal Desires

Use journaling to explore your personal desires for a romantic relationship. Consider both spiritual and practical aspects.

Step 3: Symbolic Self-Love Gestures

Symbolize your commitment to self-love with gestures, such as gifting yourself flowers or playfully embracing the idea of a self-marriage.

Step 4: Collaborative Love Map Creation

Partner with a friend or someone you trust, and together, create a collaborative Love Map that represents your collective visions for love.

Step 5: Creative Expression

Use markers, essential oils, and any other creative tools to express your desires visually on the board.

Step 6: Positive Infusion

Infuse the board with positive energy by focusing on the joy and fulfillment you anticipate in your future romantic relationship.

Step 7: Visualization and Manifestation

Use visualization techniques to imagine the presence of your ideal partner. Picture the manifestation of your sacred partnership and imagine the feeling that would come from having this type of love. Visualize your map coming to life.

Step 8: Essential Oil and Affirmation Ritual

Select essential oils that resonate with you and hold sacred significance, especially those known for love and connection, such as Joy, Abundance or Build Your Dream. Say affirmations using essential oils, affirming your worthiness of sacred love.

Step 9: Realign with Shared Values

Use this practice to recenter and realign with your life values and intentions. Release it and let it go. Put the map out of sight for several weeks.

CHAPTER 17

The Rainbow Road

"The world is full of magic things, patiently waiting
for our senses to grow sharper."
— W.B. YEATS

IFE tends to reveal its full manifestation when we are ready
to welcome and incorporate life lessons and spiritual
truths. In my case, this integration came after six months of
dedicated prayer and meditation as I navigated a challenging
divorce. Others may experience this through various life tran-
sitions, such as illness, shifts in career, or the dissolution of
friendships. Essentially, it can come through any experience
that gives us the opportunity to move inward, explore the
shadows of our existence and to choose love over fear. In my
case, the process of integration was enhanced with the support of therapists, friends, and coaches. In addition to that, I
enrolled in courses aimed at healing from emotional and financial trauma, driven by a determination to extract meaning
and personal growth from the challenges I encountered.

Following the coursework and therapeutic healing, I col-
laborated with other energy healers, broadening my network.

I also embraced the use of "I AM" affirmations as a practice to reinforce the spiritual truths revealed to me during this time.

During this period, I found myself called to new lands for work events and soaked up the lessons I was meant to experience at each of these sacred sites. I started hosting more retreats, connecting to different ley lines — a term referring to alignments of geographical points that are believed to have spiritual significance and often associated with special energy or power. As I did so, I traveled to ancient sites linked by these ley lines. Of all the places I traveled to, Hawaii is the place that showed me the "Rainbow Road" — where life aligns in a way that feels magical, serendipitously meeting the right contact or catching every green light when you are running late. It's where everything falls into place with perfect timing.

My connection to the land in Hawaii felt like pure magic, and this enchantment planted its roots years before. It began when I visited with my family to celebrate my fortieth birthday, a time when I was still married. I still remember the excitement we all felt as we landed on the island. The kids were overjoyed, and I felt as though I had been waiting my whole life to get there.

As I hiked across a lava field and completed the trail through a rainforest on that first day in Hawaii, a vision unfolded before me. It felt like walking on another planet, transitioning from the dry, hard, cracked expanse of the lava field to the lush and rich landscape of the forest part of the hike. My children continued walking ahead, and I fell behind in silence, embracing the magic that enveloped me.

As I walked, I sensed a kingly presence that seemed to walk alongside me, providing a calming and grounding energy. The king was dressed in white with gold and blue accents, wearing a very tall headpiece. Despite not recognizing who he represented or knowing anything about Hawaiian history, I stood in awe, welcoming the familiar warm energy emanating from him.

Through his thoughts, he communicated with me and sent me a message, *"You will return to Hawaii within a year, and you will continue to come back regularly."*

Initially, I dismissed the message, thinking that it was impossible to consider another trip after waiting for forty years and spending so much money on my birthday trip. I loved the place so much that I thought it was just wishful thinking. However, moments later, a queenly energy entered the space on my right side. I felt her warmth, validating the king's message. As I walked along, I absorbed the powerful presences of the two beings and felt the Earth supporting me. The magic of the moment moved through me, and I expressed gratitude before letting it go and catching up with the children.

To my amazement, the vision I had experienced became a reality. Within a few months, I found myself at the top of the oils business I had started and was rewarded with an all-expense-paid trip to the Big Island, the same place I had visited earlier. I returned to Kona within the year and even won another trip to Hawaii through my oils business a year later. The vision had indeed come true, and it opened up many opportunities for me to visit Hawaii, which became an integral part of my spiritual journey.

Over the course of four years, I had the privilege of visiting Kona four times, each time witnessing the magic I felt upon arriving. I consider Hawaii to be "The Bowl of Light," a term borrowed from Hank Weisselman's book that beautifully captures the spiritual essence of the land.

My connection to the Rainbow Road in Hawaii continued to manifest when I facilitated a retreat with LeeYen Anderson, an amazingly compassionate soul sister and healer. Together, we guided a transformative spiritual retreat in the heart of the Big Island.

One summer day in 2021, the Universe nudged me to connect with LeeYen, and affirmed what we had known for a while — that we would work together. The announcement of two new essential oils blends, "I AM Blessed" and "I AM Creative," felt like a nod toward the spiritual practice I'd developed over the previous two years. As you're aware, during that time, I had diligently recited "I AM" affirmations multiple times daily.

I strongly believed that these blends possessed the potential to bring about significant shifts in people's lives, helping them align with their true paths and elevate their vibrational frequency. This time, I listened to Source and acted quickly. Before the announcement of the two oils was over, I received a message from my Presence to reach out to

LeeYen and propose the idea of a retreat centered around this oils collection. Within seconds, the vision was set into motion. We planned a 21-day meditation journey focused on the oils, which closed with an in-person retreat in the magical setting of Hawaii.

In the week leading up to the retreat, I had a recurring dream where I heard the words: "*As Above, So Below*."

I understood the dreams to mean that one mission for the retreat was to bring Heaven to Earth, and the power of our purpose was palpable.

We held our "Sanctuary of Light" retreat overlooking *Ke ala ke kua*, which in Hawaiian means "The God's Pathway." This "pathway," according to sacred geometry, is a very powerful vortex. The retreat center we rented, The Whale Spirit Sanctuary property, is in direct alignment with this vortex and gave our retreat an extra oomph of mana, healing, and rejuvenation.

The land was sacred in other qualities as well. There were pools of water nearby that were said to hold water sources fueled by both Sacred Masculine and Sacred Feminine energy. There was a sacred site at the foot of the hill where we stayed that inspired the visions of Wesselman's book.

The attendees consisted of a diverse group of healers, ranging from those new to their practice to seasoned practitioners. We extended invitations to exceptional facilitators, and among them was my close friend, Kris Olivas, an integrative therapist, energy and shamanic healer. Kris and I traveled from California to the retreat together, and from the outset, it felt as though we were being guided by something far bigger than ourselves. I was familiar with this kind of energy, as whenever Kris and I come together, there's a distinct amplification of positive energy, whether we're working collaboratively or simply navigating the world side by side.

The day of the trip, happiness surrounded us at every turn. The way things unfolded felt like a guided experience, which I like to call the "Rainbow Road." The airport staff greeted us with smiles, and it felt as if the crowds cleared the way. A new lined developed just as we entered the check-in line, moving through security was a breeze, and we walked straight to the gate just as it was time to board. Any needs we had were promptly taken care of, and the pre-trip stress melted away, giving way to ease and joy.

I remember during our layover, that the pre-flight Covid line had no wait and I even got a free latte from one of the cafes. Kris, who was attending and facilitating our retreat, and she and I spoke excitedly on the flight. The flight went by so fast. The experience began the moment our plane took off, and I could feel the energy lift us up.

Kris and I laughed about how effortlessly the day went, a sentiment made even more remarkable considering we were traveling during the pandemic. Every moment of the journey was deeply appreciated, and the Rainbow Road seemed to guide us with ease and joy.

Source energy expanded even more upon arrival. I sensed

it again as soon as I set foot on the land. On that first day, we meditated on the beach at the bottom of the hill where our retreat took place, in the exact place where Hank Wesselman had received the visions detailed in his book "The Bowl of Light." As we meditated, I sat on a large tree trunk and went inward and had a mystical experience of my own. Suddenly I connected to the birds and discovered a new spiritual skill intricately linked to sound healing.

As I mentioned earlier, ever since waking from the coma, I have been able to feel music in my body as I hear it. These days, whether it is live music or recorded, I can feel the chords and melody moving along my spine, neck, arms, shoulders, and even in my heart space. Until that meditation, this had only happened when listening to live or recorded music. But on that day, as I became fully present, I felt the birds singing in my body.

After this powerful experience I was curious to explore this more. On the second day, as I listened to the sounds of the birds, I became mesmerized by the sensations that swept through my body. What other frequencies could I tune into? What could I learn from the natural world around me?

Driven by these questions, I made it my mission to experience the waves in the same way. I meditated on the beach over the next two days but I couldn't seem to get it right. My usual techniques of tuning in to the sound didn't seem to work with the rhythmic ebb and flow of the waves.

I practiced surrendering control and releasing it to Source.

However, I didn't develop the skill until we led the group in an evening meditation a couple of days later. This meditation took place by the ocean on sacred land.

We walked onto the beach in silence, my sole intention being to feel the waves in my body. As I sat down, I felt a powerful protective energy gathering around me, almost as if giants had entered the space. However, they weren't angry, only curious. I communicated with them that I was there to feel the waves and asked if we could stay for a short while. They allowed it and moved back, and the vibrations of the space opened to me. I focused my attention on the waves once more.

I released all control and expectation and asked for guidance. I received a message to expand awareness of my energy. In that moment, I let my focus shift from feeling sensations in my human body to the energetic field that exists outside of my human form.

This energetic field exists about four to six inches beyond the edges of my physical body. As I expanded my awareness to this area, I could feel the waves strongly in my energetic field. It was like a light switch had been turned on!

Suddenly, I felt intense sensations up and down my spine, similar to those I feel when I listen to music. The waves hit me in a new way, moving not only up and down my spine but also across my shoulders, creating a highly rhythmic sensory experience. Although it felt delightful, it intensified to the point where it bordered on discomfort, signaling a strong activation within me.

I tried not to get too excited that I had unlocked this awareness. I didn't want to slip into my thinking mind. I sat fully present as I experienced the waves, letting them cleanse my energetic body as I meditated. It was magical, and it helped me understand that nature can provide the same type of energetic support as the light on the other side, echoing the wisdom from my recurring dreams of "As Above, So Below."

With Anela's guidance, we continued to create rituals to express gratitude for the blessings of the sacred land. We were rewarded with enchanting phenomena in the land and sky. We saw rainbow reflections after our workshops, as well as small, triangular rainbows in the clouds. We saw an inverted rainbow above the lanai in our retreat space just after we completed a workshop where we connected to the sound of our souls through the singing bowls. We saw unique cloud structures, and one of our participants was able to see temples in the clouds above the land. The sun created unique shapes as it beamed down over the ocean, and we even saw a golden pathway leading to it. We marveled over the light anomalies and got the message that we should follow them to find our sacred snorkeling spot.

On the third day, we arranged to go snorkeling, and were delighted to points of light in the water, leading us to a sacred underwater sanctuary. It was a place we knew was special, which is why we chose to snorkel there. The light anomalies appeared as different sized spheres of light that formed a pathway in the water in front of us.

The day before we went snorkeling, I shared a download-
ed message about points of light, a message that had come to
me came to me like this: Each cell within us contains a point
of light. In fact, everything we see is made up of these tiny
points. We can train ourselves to notice them by focusing on
wet or shiny objects, where it's easier to observe them.

Developing the skill of seeing these points of light in everything is truly amazing. Learning how to see them is a simple
technique: when looking at something wet, pull back perception to see if you can notice something resembling glitter in
the wetness. Continually pulling back and softening the gaze
reveals the "glistening" as countless tiny points of light. When
you master this skill, everything can be perceived in this way,
giving the world a kind of backlit glow. Everything — absolutely everything — is made of light.

Seeing the points of light leading our boat was a delightful experience for everyone. Shouts of joy filled the air as we
observed the light-pathway in front of us and we asked the
captain to follow them. We knew they were leading us somewhere magical. Upon reaching the snorkel spot, each of us
encountered something in the water. For me, it was out of
this world — something that I know I will never see again in
this lifetime.

I remember snorkeling to the outer edge of the cove and
submerging myself in the water. When I opened my eyes, I
saw a mesmerizing sight: a wall of beautiful fish staring back
at me. They were suspended in the water, floating in stillness,

and there were hundreds of them, each in different colors and sizes. Time felt like it had stopped as they all seemed to fixate on me. In that moment, I felt their wisdom, and my heart swelled with compassion for their beautiful presence and the profound gift they were offering. I felt the presence of God in that moment.

The points of light guided me to those fish to share a beautiful message that carried a powerful lesson: *all beings are connected.* It reminded me that in life, there are these guiding Points of Light leading us toward sacred and transformative experiences. Perhaps we just need to learn to recognize them.

It was also a reminder of the power and presence of Mother Earth. During this experience with the fish, I felt Heaven on Earth: *As Above, So Below!*

Just as music connects me to the place of light, signs and sounds of nature can also connect us. This became a recurring theme during the rest of the retreat, with each workshop gaining more spiritual energy. It felt like we had brought heavenly experiences down to earth, and everything was fitting together perfectly.

The energy grew more every hour, culminating in the final evening of the retreat. At the final workshop, we invited all participants to come together to share gifts in a blessing circle. Each of us took turns in the center of the circle while the others sent blessings through hands, musical instruments, voice, or movement. The experience was about five minutes or so for each person, but time seemed to stop as we each took our place in the center of the circle. It was one of the most transcendent moments in my life, and I felt so connected that I almost left my body, tempted to linger in the light realm once again.

As it became my turn to step into the blessing circle, I felt once again that I was guided by something greater. The air was charged with intensity as I floated towards the center of the circle. Lying down on the table, I closed my eyes and immediately felt myself lift out of my body.

Lightness washed over me and I saw a vision of an Ascended Master with kind and loving eyes, someone I had been hoping to see for years, but who had not yet come to me. His face before me was magnificent. I was surrounded by light once again, but this time, there were unfamiliar symbols in the air that moved through me so quickly, I could barely see them. Despite my lack of understanding, I had a deep sense that they held some kind of wisdom that was being unlocked within me.

In the midst of savoring the beauty of that moment, my conscious mind recognized that I had stopped breathing. It was at that point I received a message to release that concern: *"You don't need to breathe; your body will be taken care of."*

Suddenly, a giant clear crystal octahedron appeared above me, with its point directed downwards. Months before this moment, I had two visions of an octahedron during meditations. The first time, it appeared as a rotating blue shape. It can best be described as a blue pyramid atop an inverse pyramid, with the points of each pyramid pointing in opposite directions and connected at the base. In the first vision, each point seemed to spin in an opposite direction, forming rotating imaginary circles above and below.

During another meditation on the cliffs overlooking the coast, the familiar shape revealed itself to me once again. This time, I envisioned a life-sized, transparent iteration of the crystal pyramid. In this coastal vision, its upper half emerged above the water's surface, while the remaining half rested beneath the water. As I remained in the moment, feeling deeply honored to witness it once again, I realized it is my personal symbol of bridging Heaven and Earth.

It felt like a gift from the heavens to see the octahedron again, and I lovingly received its blessing and energy while in Hawaii. This was the moment when my soul lifted out of my body, with that all-familiar euphoric reconnection with the light. I was back in the light again, completely immersed in the energy. A sense of complete wholeness moved through me. Although I was still aware that my human body wasn't breathing, I knew that my body didn't need it and that I would be entirely cared for.

The experience of leaving my physical body to join my Higher Presence in the light was different from my NDE. The space in which I found myself was difficult to describe, with a light turquoise color unlike anything I had seen before. It wasn't the intensely bright golden light from my NDE, but something otherworldly. The turquoise became so faint that it almost appeared white, as if it was a color not meant for human eyes. The atmosphere was charged with an electric energy, and I felt a deep sense of love and absolute connection to creation.

Yet, in one striking similarity to my near-death experience, I felt whole, connected, at peace, and reunited.

I had the thought that I didn't want to go back to my human body. To this, I heard the words:

"You still have work to do."

At the exact moment I heard those words, one of our participants firmly grabbed on to my ankles, having received her own message to bring me back into my physical form. I drew myself back to Earth. I sensed the constricting energy as I returned to my body and opened my eyes. The entire circle of participants provided support as I shook violently upon re-entering my body. We chose to pause the next part of the circle, as I needed time to ground myself and regain composure.

I was left with an overwhelming sense of gratitude and wonder. While I may never fully comprehend the significance of what happened, I know that it was a gift. It has reminded me to remain open and to have faith in the timing of the divine. Though I attended the retreat with the intention of giving, I left with the realization that when we give of ourselves, we open to receiving as well. This was an important lesson for me, and one that I will carry with me throughout my life.

I was informed afterward that the energy in the room shifted while I was in the center. This validated that the experience was not just for me, but for the entire group. It was an honor to have played a role in such a transformative and powerful experience.

These mystical and validating experiences of Hawaii are not just stories, but act as a gateway to the inherent wisdom and intuition within. May they remind you to recognize the wisdom of your own personal life experiences. The exercises woven into each chapter of this book also serve a greater purpose: to empower you in tapping into the wellspring of intuition and divine connection that resides within you.

Now that you've read about these meaningful experiences and completed the exercises to sharpen your intuition, think about what comes next on your journey. Come back to these exercises as tools in your spiritual toolbox along with the things you've picked up during our shared exploration.

As you finish reading this book, picture the road ahead — one where spirituality and the real world blend seamlessly. Trust your ability to understand the messages the universe is sending you, and let it help you create your own version of a happy life.

May the messages in this book serve as stepping stones guiding you towards a life attuned to the energies of the world. Embrace the idea of being a conscious creator. May your path be lit by the wisdom of intuition that will shape a reality in alignment with the special energies you've discovered.

May you live on the Rainbow Road.

✳ ✳ ✳

CLOSING MEDITATION

Embracing Your Intuitive Path

Step 1: Set the Stage

Find a quiet space where you can be undisturbed, whether indoors or outdoors. Assume a comfortable position, ensuring you are fully present for this closing ritual.

Step 2: Gratitude for the Journey

Commence the closing ritual by taking several deep breaths, expressing gratitude for the transformative journey you've undertaken. Acknowledge the gifts of wisdom and intuition you've uncovered throughout this exploration.

Step 3: Connection to Inner Wisdom

Reflect on the interconnectedness of your journey with the wisdom you've discovered within yourself. Consider the experiences as symbolic companions on your path. Sense the profound connection between your insights and the inner realms of your being.

Step 4: Acknowledging Your Presence

Engage in a simple ritual to acknowledge your presence in this moment. This could involve a grounding gesture, such as placing your hands on your heart or quietly affirming your identity as you continue to explore your intuitive abilities.

Step 5: Integration of Insights

Close your eyes and bring to mind the insights and wisdom gained during your experiences. Let these revelations integrate into your being, recognizing the resonance between your intuitive self and the harmonious energies within you.

Step 6: Expressing Thanks

Express gratitude for the guidance and support received throughout this journey. Thank your intuitive self and the insights that have accompanied you. Acknowledge the co-creative process that has unfolded, allowing you to shape your reality in alignment with your inner wisdom.

Step 7: Closing Gesture

Conclude the closing ritual with a simple gesture that signifies the closure of this chapter. This could be placing your hands on your heart, a nod of acknowledgment, or whispering a word of thanks. Know that you carry the tools and insights acquired during this exploration into your everyday life. Whenever you seek to reconnect with the profound energies of intuition, remember this ritual as a guide on your continued journey.

Acknowledgments

THIS JOURNEY to share my Near Death Experience and spiritual insights through writing has been an adventure, made possible by the collective wisdom, encouragement, and support of some truly remarkable individuals.

I'm deeply grateful to Jack Canfield for his mentorship and inspiration, which guided me to embark on this journey of writing and self-exploration. His encouragement to simply begin with "just 80 pages" has led me through a transformative process, where the act of writing itself became a pathway to discovering depths and facets of my story I hadn't anticipated.

The heart of this book's clarity and depth comes from the collective editing prowess of Chris Haden, Jennifer Bauer, Debra Root, and Tracy Bucchare. Their meticulous work has deeply enhanced this narrative, and for that, my gratitude is immense.

I also want to recognize the facilitators who have significantly contributed to the dialogues within this book — LeeYen Anderson, Anela Watson, Kris Olivas, Lorna Christensen, Jeanine Albert, Emilia Nagy, and many others. Their dedication to fostering growth and enlightenment in others has been truly inspiring. Additionally, I'm grateful for the thought leaders before me whose work has shaped our path of exploration and discovery.

Acknowledgments are also due to Alysha Suley, Tracy Walton, and Bobbi Jo Etheridge. Their contributions, read-throughs, and suggestions have enriched this journey in countless ways.

Beverly Haney's artistic talent merits individual acclaim. Through her adept graphic design, she's masterfully encapsulated the essence of my near-death experience on the cover, offering a visual that is both stunningly beautiful and remarkably accurate.

To my beloved family — my parents, who instilled in me the courage to pursue my dreams and showed me the meaning of unconditional love; my siblings and extended family for their unwavering support; and most importantly, my children, from whom I've learned the depths of love and the joy of living authentically. Your belief in me has been my guiding light.

Neil, my Love, your belief in my dreams has transformed the impossible into reality. Your love, support and encouragement have been my sanctuary. Thank you for being the love that inspires every word I share.

Immense thanks to Lilia Samolia, my mentor, whose sage advice and spiritual insights have significantly shaped the direction and essence of my life and this work. Your guidance has been a cornerstone of my spiritual expansion.

To my friends, Audrey Van Alyea and Samantha Annuzzi,

who have been havens of comfort, joy, and inspiration along the way. Your support and camaraderie have been a beacon in moments of doubt and celebration alike.

This book also honors my clients, whose own magic and openness in sessions have not only facilitated this work but added a richness and depth to it. Your willingness to embark on this journey with me has been a gift, allowing for a shared exploration of spiritual healing and connection.

Lastly, I am eternally grateful for the Divine Presence, the ultimate source of inspiration, reminding me of the interconnectedness of all life and the beauty inherent in our shared human experience.

This book stands as a testament to everyone who has walked this path with me, who has shared in the laughter and the tears, and who has contributed in countless ways, both big and small. Your support and belief in this endeavor have been the guiding stars, illuminating my journey through both the challenges and triumphs. This acknowledgment serves as a mirror of my gratitude for each of you and your indispensable roles in this narrative.

www.ingramcontent.com/pod-product-compliance
Lightning Source LLC
Chambersburg PA
CBHW020452130626
46549CB00001B/388